## Author Information

Tony Clayton-Lea is an award-winning freelance journalist/editor who specialises in rock music, film and travel for a variety of publications, including *The Irish Times* and *Cara Magazine*. He has written four music-related books and lives in County Meath with Angela and their two teenagers, Paul and Sarah.

# Essential Irish Rock Quotes

Tony Clayton-Lea

The Collins Press

PUBLISHED IN 2008 BY
The Collins Press
West Link Park
Doughcloyne
Wilton
Cork

British Library Cataloguing in Publication Data
  Rockaganda : essential Irish rock quotes
  1. Rock music - Ireland - Quotations, maxims, etc. 2. Rock
  musicians - Ireland - Quotations
  I. Clayton-Lea, Tony
  781.6'6'09415
  ISBN-13: 9781905172764

Typesetting by The Collins Press
Typeset in Bembo 11 on 14 pt
Printed in Great Britain by
CPI Cox & Wyman, Reading, RG1 8EX

*To Nicholas, Anne and the two Pauls — one brother, one son.*

# CONTENTS

# Rockaganda

# ACKNOWLEDGEMENTS

It takes more than one person to cobble together a book such as this; for starters, there is The Collins Press who gave the project structure and shape. There is the Literary Agent who deals with the nitty-gritty – Chelsey Fox. There are the many, many publications, magazines and writers whose work I have yet again filleted for quotes (special mention, however, has to go to George Byrne, whose series of the 'Worst Dublin Bands In The World . . . Ever' in *In Dublin* magazine in the mid-1990s provided some of the book's funniest moments). Also thanks to Marcus Connaughton for unearthing interviews with Rory Gallagher, and to Wayne Cronin for (literally) digging up a couple of *D'Side* magazines. Finally – and, as always – massive thanks to my family for their grace in allowing me the time to work on such an undertaking.

Tony Clayton-Lea

July 2008

# SEX

It occupies our minds for more minutes than we care to admit; if you're a rock star, however, sex becomes wrapped up – if you will, cling-filmed – in the music to the extent that it often overtakes the medium. Back in the 1950s, when this entire rock 'n' roll lark effectively started (although let us not forget that a decade earlier Frank Sinatra had the bobby soxers moist around the ankles), sex was a comparatively innocent wiggle of the hips. Since then, morals have changed radically, and the sexualisation of music has become all-pervasive, a fact that justifiably concerns parents when they see their nine-year old daughters dress up like one of The Pussycat Dolls. Yet sex is intrinsically associated with rock music for a fairly obvious reason – it is primarily a primal thing that is rooted in the body's rhythms, something that's unavoidable in the case of Thin Lizzy guitar solos, the nuances of Divine Comedy and the grind of Therapy?, but less obvious, perhaps, in the back catalogue of Mary Black.

❖

'I don't fancy any of The Corrs. They're all beautiful but . . . too much blusher.'
*Sinéad O'Connor,* Q *(November 2000)*

'Showbands were about music and entertainment in much the same way that Bewley's was about coffee. Fundamentally, they were about sex, about meeting, romancing and mating, and about extending to the first Irish pop generation the kind of freedom purveyed in the international arena by Elvis, Dylan and the Beatles.'
*John Waters,* The Irish Times *(January 2008)*

'Is there anybody here with any Irish in them? Is there any of the girls who'd like a little more Irish in them?'
*Thin Lizzy's Phillip Lynott, as quoted in* Mojo *(December 1993)*

'I wrote a song called "Much More Than This", and in it I discuss the possibility that when you're alone and away from home and somebody tries to seduce you in a hotel room – if you fall for it, how will that affect things with your loved one? My point is that you shouldn't break up a relationship because you spent a night with a person under severe loneliness and stress . . . If a marriage breaks up because one of the partners has been unfaithful once, then the marriage doesn't deserve to stick together. It's absurd for people to break up because of that. There are far more important things that will test a relationship than one-night infidelities. Whatever your moral viewpoint on this, or your views on monogamy, the most important thing is a spiritual bond between you and your loved one and that should transcend anything.'

*Chris de Burgh,* Hot Press *(1 December 1988)*

'I'm a big romance person. I love the old-fashionedness of it, the simple things that are not reflected upon enough, that get neglected because sex is always in your face. Sex is overrated ... When you're having sex, you're having a great time and not thinking. You're like, whoo and whoah; the mental camera is not going, you're just indulging. It's like pigging out on a cake and you can't remember belching afterwards.'

*Dolores O'Riordan,* Q *(May 1996)*

'Far more than Gay Byrne or Nell McCafferty or David Norris or Mary Robinson, men like Joe Dolan revolutionized Irish attitudes to, in a word, sex.'

*John Waters,* The Irish Times *(January 2008)*

'I'm aware that it's [Rastafarianism] anti-gay in a lot of ways. I can deal with that even though I'm a woman who likes shagging birds. I'm also madly in love with a man right now. Which makes me bisexual, I guess.'

*Sinéad O'Connor,* Uncut *(July 2007)*

'On Hallowe'en night 1975, having learned "Burnin'" by Bob Marley and Dr Feelgood's "Down By The Jetty", we played this college as The Nightlife Thugs. It began with sheer terror, but when the clapping started filtering through it was extraordinary. In the break, two things happened: a beautiful girl came over and said, "I want to fuck you", and I rubbed "The Nightlife Thugs" off the blackboard with the full confidence that this girl gave me, and wrote "The Boomtown Rats", which I got out of Woody Guthrie's "Bound For Glory". And I did shag the beautiful girl that night.'

*Bob Geldof,* Mojo *(May 2004)*

'I'd a very innocent upbringing. It was very late in life when I swopped football for an interest in girls. I remained a virgin until I was nineteen and I don't think I french-kissed anyone until I was sixteen. And I don't think I was unique. When I was finishing my Leaving Cert in James Street, there was nobody in the class who'd lost his virginity . . . I thought that was normal. It wasn't as if we were trying to lose it, we just didn't have any interest. Nobody knew they had it to lose! I was kept away from women for a very long time by the Christian Brothers, so I'd say I am slightly in awe of them a bit. But I do find them very . . . attractive. One of the things that really pisses me off about the Christian Brothers is that they convinced me that girls don't like sex, and I really feel aggrieved about that.'

*Something Happens frontman, Tom Dunne,* Hot Press *(28 June 1990)*

'People consider me pretty, so I might as well say it, but I used to get hit on by these creeps. Old men. Just because

I was nice they'd end up saying the most disgusting things to me. And frighten me. Sexually provocative things. And when you're a young girl that's frightening. You had to realise that you had to be on your guard. I don't think women always think of the possibility of it. Sometimes I look at women and think why are you doing that? Just because you haven't ever been attacked doesn't mean it can't happen. That's why I stay away until I know someone is okay.'

*Sharon Corr, Q (July 1999)*

'We dabbled with sexual politics in a very subversive way in the Virgin Prunes, but it was never drag, never pom-poms and peacocks. Sometimes you get tired of hearing about high heels, tit jobs and wigs. You know, I love the theatre of it, and a lot of trannies look amazing, but spend an hour with them and . . . well.'

*Gavin Friday, Mojo (March 1996)*

'Fidelity is just against human nature. That's where we have to either engage or not engage our higher side . . . It's like in school when they tell you about drugs – "If you smoke drugs you'll become an addict and you'll die the next week." They don't tell you even half the truth. I think the same is true about sex. You know, if you tell people that the best place to have sex is in the safe hands of a loving relationship, you may be telling a lie! There may be other places. If the question is, can I as a married man write about sex with a stranger, "yes" has got to be the answer. I've got to write about that because that is part of the subject I'm writing about. You have to try and expose some myths, even if they expose you along the way. I don't want to talk about my own relationship, because I've too much respect for Ali to do so. What I'm saying to you is, I may or may not be writing from my own experience on some of these, but that doesn't make it any less real.'

*Bono*, U2: At the End of the World *by Bill Flanagan (Bantam Press 1995)*

'There's nothing wrong with a bit of good old non-penetrative sex, all forms of sexuality are equally attractive. But I don't think you'll ever convince people not to make love.'

*Sinéad O'Connor*, Hot Press *(12 December 1991)*

'When one of my schoolmates was teaching me how to wank. I was twelve and I must have been the only boy in the world who had to be taught to wank. But I mastered it pretty quickly and never looked back.'

*Bob Geldof on being asked what was the closest he ever came to having a homosexual experience,* Q *(January 1995)*

ADAM CLAYTON: 'I'd have to say that within the U2 camp, I would definitely be the most diminutive of all the members.'

# Sex

EDGE: 'Adam is the most well endowed member, no contest, but he wouldn't know because he's blind.'

BONO: 'Some people think U2 should be hung. All I am saying is that we are, in fact, particularly well hung.'

*Locker room chat,* U2 by U2 *(October 2006)*

'What is your most treasured possession?'

'My willie!'

*Adam Clayton,* Zoo TV *Tour Programme (1992)*


'I love women, they're definitely the stronger sex. Some of my best friends are women. Some of my best friends dress up as women, too.'

*Bono,* Hot Press *(December 1988)*


'I was shy about women and drinking got me past first base – but the post-match reports wouldn't be generous.'

*Ash's Rick McMurray,* Q *(June 2001)*


'Rhythm is the sex of music. If U2 is to explore erotic themes we have to have sexuality in the music as well as the words.'

*Bono,* U2: At the End of the World *by Bill Flanagan (Bantam Press 1995)*


'Women were ringing him every day. One day I was in the house . . . when the doorbell rang at 11 a.m. Phil was in his room, so I answered the door and there was this nice-looking woman with a bottle of whiskey in her hand. Is Philip here? she says. So I ask her name and went

7

in, shouted up to Phil and he says, Send her up. That happened three times one day.'

*One-time member of Thin Lizzy, Robbie Brennan, Mojo (December 1993)*

'Stupid, stupid, absolutely stupid. If I could change anything, I would change saying that. I made an idiot of myself, but listen, I was sixteen years of age. I did mean it, I thought it was alright saying it. What a fucking idiot. Gobshite is the word. I knew nothing sexual-education wise, I was giggling at the back of the class. I was into sports, I loved cars and I never had girlfriends. I wasn't that way oriented. I was more into listening to music, playing football and hanging out. And I was starting to drink, so I was hanging out with me mates in bars. I'd be talking about girls, but I was still very naive to that whole situation, I swear to God.'

*Ronan Keating, on announcing that he would remain a virgin until his wedding night, Q (September 2000)*

# DRUGS/DRINK

In the same way that sex is inextricably linked with rock music, so too are drugs and alcohol. Most of us like a drink, and it's a given that at some point in our lives we will be (or, indeed, have been) so drunk we can't remember the night before and shudder to think what the day ahead is going to be like. Rock stars (genuine and wannabe) and rock music fans have all tasted the socio-cultural drip-fed honey of alcohol; a percentage have been able to leave it at that and go about their business without feeling the need to take it to the limit. Others, of course, have succumbed to what is either (depending on where your instincts lie) a truism or a myth: that coming close to or going over the edge in the intake of alcohol and/or narcotics brings you closer to the hub of creativity; that the link between commonplace cleverness and genius is to be found in copious amounts of cocktails. Some rock stars have discovered that, in the long run, all those years spent chasing spurious notions of creative greatness as they were looking at life through the bottom of a glass might have been better used. Other rock stars are inexorably sucked into a stale-smelling and stained void of their own making and find they are unable to claw their way back out. Which begs the questions: what price should you pay for creative enlightenment? And if there's any change out of a tenner, would you buy a bag of crisps?

'The thing that hindered the creative juices was the whole drug scene. They took too big a bite out of us and left us hollow. They [hard drugs] didn't really come in until after the *Black Rose* album and it only got really heavy in the last three years. We talked about it all the time. We'd say to each other, we've got to get off this shit. But in the same breath it was, where are we gonna score?'

*Thin Lizzy's Scott Gorham on Phil Lynott,* Mojo *(December 1993)*

'Certainly there was a time when I felt I couldn't do a gig without drinking. I used to be very nervous and I did drink way too much, but now I just go up to my local for two pints and that's enough for me.'

*Mary Coughlan,* Hot Press *(22 March 1990)*

'Crash Course To Oblivion.'

*Shane MacGowan tells us the title of a possible autobiography,* Q *(February 1993)*

'Like an idiot I gave him £600. Then I went to see him . . . And found he'd spent it on heroin. He pulled out this bag of smack in front of me and did it . . . I told him, you do that and I'm going to the fucking police! And I'll shop him a zillion times if I have to. In my opinion, Shane MacGowan is dangerous. To himself and others . . . I hoped being arrested he would be forced into treatment. He has tried to stop on his own but cannot. He is incapable of functioning on any level if someone doesn't lift him out of the hell he has himself locked up in. As soon as you go in the door (of his flat), the smell of puke hits you. The carpet is black and rotten. Bottles everywhere. No food in the fridge. All he eats is Marks & Spencer's tiramisu.'

*Sinéad O'Connor, on reporting The Pogues singer to the UK police,* Q *(March 2000)*

'He was very angry at the time. He did do a few sulky interviews and quite dishonestly said that I was there in my priest gear ordering him that he had to obey me. Come on, like, are you fucking mental? But he's now subsequently been going around saying that actually I did save his life. He's now not on smack, but he's on enough morphine to kill an elephant. But he would have been dead if I hadn't done it. That's the truth, like, and he knows that. I didn't want to be singing at his fucking funeral.'

*Sinéad O'Connor on the same topic,* Mojo *(October 2005)*

'Sinéad did me a favour. I was furious at the time but I'm eternally grateful to her now.'

*Shane MacGowan, ditto,* The Word *(January 2005)*

'I haven't done drugs in at least ten years. Forget it! I did coke on the tours and soon that ended up boring me. You sound like such an arsehole on it. And someone, instead of giving me coke, once gave me smack and that nearly killed me so that was the end of that. But then I'm not an addictive personality. I don't drink much. Don't smoke. Jaysus. I'm beginning to sound like Saint Bob now!'

*Bob Geldof,* Hot Press *(December 1989)*

'I was as bad and mad as everyone else, and wasn't an easy guy to be around when I was loaded.'

*Terry Woods,* The Irish Times *(August 2002)*

'Being Shane, not much went to plan. He was dropped off by his road manager, Charlie McLennan, very late and absolutely hammered. He was yawning, smoking and sort of dribbling – he had swollen ankles and no socks – and he'd passed out after we dressed him up. We only had three hours so we had to set up around him and shoot while he was unconscious. Eventually he came round and was actually very helpful and mild-mannered, though he didn't say much.'

*Photographer Andy Solomon, on 'shooting' Pogues singer Shane MacGowan for the French music magazine* Best, Mojo *(January 2007)*

'Why do people expect us to solve the world's problems? It's absurd. I mean, if politicians can't do it, how the hell can musicians? You have to go back to the Sixties, when people were smoking dope and getting high and listening to things and perceiving things that weren't actually true.

That's where all that came from. I suppose, also, that journalists were getting stoned and doing the same thing. It's another myth: "What does it mean?" You can see all sorts of things if you're drugged up, you can read anything into anything.'

*Van Morrison,* Q *(April 1997)*

'Adam didn't have any partners in crime in the band, so some of the people he ended up hanging out with were dodgy – road warriors who had been around the block . . . I mean, the band weren't even drinking. Can you imagine?! You're in a candy store and these guys don't even want to smell the sweets. Strange days indeed.'

*Larry Mullen Jr,* U2 by U2 *(October 2006)*

'Here was a man you could trust with your life. But suddenly here's a man on hard drugs. I felt uneasy around him. He was rambling, incoherent, unpredictable, violent, moody and just not the same person I knew at all. I would say to him, C'mon, let's get you healthy, let's get you moving, let's get you to a hospital. And where before he would take that as good advice, he would take it as sticking my nose in where it didn't belong.'

*Irish artist Jim Fitzpatrick on Phil Lynott,* Mojo *(December 1993)*

'I've had a go at them all, really . . . I smoked all the time for about ten years. Literally all the time. Every day. For a while, then, in the late Sixties and early Seventies, I did a

fair bit of acid. I couldn't handle it all now. I'd be terrified of it now. I wouldn't recommend it, to be honest . . . And the mushrooms . . . I'd be a bit afraid of those boys, too . . . I'm effectively off the drink now . . . I used to drink far too much. I used to go on stage drunk . . . The big thing with drink is that it's so time absorbing. It's very easy to spend six or seven hours a day drinking. It's bloody hard work, y'know?'
*Christy Moore,* Hot Press *(15 June 1984)*

'My father blames all our troubles on me smoking dope! I see that as a denial of my actual experience.'
*Sinéad O'Connor,* Q *(September 1994)*

'We drank like fishes? Well, that much is true – we did drink an awful lot. I'm neither proud of it nor ashamed of it. I'm not going to beat myself over the back with it, because that's the way it was. We did a lot of shouting and roaring and all that stuff, but you grow out of these things, to an extent. I still meet people now who are my age, which is well into my sixties, who believe those days are still here and they're still looking for the party. Well, they're over, pal. They're past.'
*Ronnie Drew, The Dubliners,* Cara Magazine *(October 2002)*

'The idea that you can't play the blues unless you're an alcoholic is nonsense, and potentially a lethal notion to be selling to young musicians . . . Sure I drink, but not to excess. And the key reason is the absolute fear of the darkness taking over. You have to step over a certain line, not necessarily to connect with evil, but to take yourself as close to the brink as you can to give the music that essential edge. It's a dangerous balance.'

*Rory Gallagher, as quoted in* Mojo *(October 1998)*

'It's one of those personal experiences that you wish the rest of the world didn't necessarily get involved in, because it's got nothing to do with the music. Nowadays the amount of people who quietly have a joint at the end of their day is a very large proportion of the population. So it's like a bit of a reality check – OK, you may live a lifestyle that is reasonably relaxed, but it's still illegal and it's illegal for an awful lot of people. You can't fuck with that aspect of the society you live in . . . for better or for worse.'

*Adam Clayton,* Q *(March 1997)*

'Shane MacGowan is unwell. In fact, he looks dead. His body is sitting on a sofa, an array of drinks set out before him – a tumbler of wine, a half-full bottle of Pinot Grigio, a Bloody Mary, some brown liquid in a glass, a scummy mug of stuff – along with three cigarette lighters, a pair of sunglasses, a cheese and tomato baguette that has seemingly been gnawed at by a passing woodland animal, and a hefty clay ashtray that has somehow come a cropper and now lies in bits on the table and the floor. It must have been some party. MacGowan is oblivious to this tableau, as he has passed out halfway into the shoulder bag that is positioned next to him. As if the effort of rummaging for, say, a fourth Clipper has exhausted his body's final reserves, he slumps there, immobile. Then, with a jolt of the shoulders and a shake of the head, his hands resume their excavation of the bag's shallow interiors. But oh no, it's all too much. He conks out again.'

The Word *(January 2005)*

'I got seriously lost in the Seventies for a while. The drink. It was beyond madness.'

*Christy Moore,* Mojo *(May 2006)*

'When I started on the road I did the whole bit, the wrecking of hotel rooms, the heavy drinking, the girls, and I smoked the odd bit of dope. But after a while you realize that you can't go on like that. Your health is the most important thing . . . I still enjoy drinking but if you overdo even that, your head starts falling apart . . . I was never interested in trying LSD. Lots of my friends did but not me. I have such wild dreams and a wild imagination that I don't want to go over the top with LSD!'

*Chris de Burgh,* Hot Press *(1 December 1988)*

'I'm not putting myself in the position of endorsing it or not. For me it has nothing to do with Rastafarianism. It's about being a rock 'n' roll chick. With two children and not liking alcohol, the best all I can get away with is a couple of spliffs. I say to my son I don't mind if he smokes a few spliffs but I'd rather he didn't do it until he's finished college. It does fuck with your mind when you start . . . I have done ecstasy three times and I fucking hate it, yeuch, disgusting. I felt like I was dying, poisoned . . . I don't

know why they call it ecstasy – they should call it Hell. But I've done LSD about seven times and I fuckin' loved it. I could happily live on it for the rest of my life, if I didn't have children and a career to be responsible for.'
*Sinéad O'Connor, Q (November 2000)*

'When we first signed to Stiff we had to pretend we'd stopped drinking. So in the photo sessions we had to hide our drinks. And in the pictures we look really miserable and uncomfortable because we're sitting on our beer cans.'
*Shane MacGowan in an excerpt from Ann Scanlon's 1988 book,* The Lost Decade, *as quoted in* The Word *(January 2005)*

'There were drugs being consumed openly, lines of cocaine on mirrors in our dressing rooms. I had no experience of drugs and judging by the people offering them to me, it was an experience I could do without.'
*Larry Mullen Jr, U2 by U2 (October 2006)*

'Drink blotted out feelings I didn't want to feel . . . That's not a problem, because you know how much you've taken, you know what it's going to do, you know how bad you'll feel the next day. I can stop any time I want. It doesn't worry me. Psychiatry? Fucking rubbish and humiliating . . . I never felt I had a major problem, but I can't actually remember much about it. What really fucked me up was mixing drinks: gin, vodka, Bacardi, then beer, then wine. I'm sticking with beer now. Another pint?'
*Ash's Mark Hamilton, Q (June 2001)*

'As soon as he opened the door I saw he was a mess — puffed out, bloated, the eyes real bloodshot. He told me, "You know, I'm gonna get my shit together, get rid of all this drug thing. I'm really gonna go for it." He actually sounded convincing, to the point where he was even talking about how we should get the band back together. But I'm looking at him thinking, Phil, you're not gonna make it, man. So we left it at that and that was literally the last time I saw him. Three weeks later I got the call — massive heart attack, intensive care, emergency hospital . . .'

*Thin Lizzy guitarist Scott Gorham on band frontman Phil Lynott,* Mojo *(February 2006)*

'Just because I smoke spliffs doesn't mean I think it's right. And saying that doesn't mean I think it's wrong, but I would not encourage my children to start smoking, nor anyone else's children. Drugs are a personal choice, similar in my mind to abortion. I feel there should be the same rules around it. Drugs should be safe and legal, and only available on prescription.'

*Sinéad O'Connor,* Hot Press *(13 February 2008)*

'The rehearsals go smoothly and quickly, so it's off to a Mexican restaurant for a chilli sensation. Michael [McKeegan, bass player] paces himself with a beer. I have two, sneak off to the toilets for some brick dust and then return for a frozen marguerita, mouth numb, head getting number. Back to the hotel room, shower, and rifle through the crumpled sports bag that is my wardrobe . . . Then it's off to Eve's in Regent Street . . . It's packed beyond comfort with bands, journos, music biz, and, apparently – someone tells me later – the vice squad. This was unknown to me, of course, as I swaggered in, swerved around a gaggle and dashed straight for the loos where I impatiently queue feigning that "I need a shit, honest" look. Wired to fuck, I head out to face the public. Teeth grinding, temples throbbing and sweating uncontrollably like a garden sprinkler, it's shake and fake time. The music's so loud I can't hear a thing anyone is saying to me. It's too hot and I'm beginning to feel restless. I could do with a shag but as I get my first come-on of the night from an expensively clothed Sloane type who, no doubt, wants my rough, workmanlike hands all over her well-bred, perfumed bod, the fear kicks in. Will the gig be good tomorrow? Will I be fit to play it? Is there blood pissing down my nose? I get out, get a cab and go to bed.'

*Therapy?'s Andy Cairns, Q (August 1995)*


'Bottom line: I think drugs are dumb. Bottom line: I think abuse of alcohol is dumb. Bottom line: I think that cigarette smoking is dumb. And that's it, really.'

Bono on Bono *(2005)*


'There were a lot of people hanging round him whom I didn't like. And most of them had a supply of amphet-amines. He'd take a hit and then he'd work for another two hours. At that stage, three a.m., I wanted to be in bed. But Phillip kept extending himself, and the only way you do that, really, is by taking something extra. And that's how it started.'

*Artist Jim Fitzpatrick on Thin Lizzy's Phil Lynott,* Mojo *(December 1993)*

'I destroyed my ego with acid. I decided to safeguard against believing my own publicity and get in touch with what's in my heart. I could see it when I was on acid or booze, but not when I was straight. Through all these people licking my arse, saying, you're wonderful . . . Fame and adulation are frightening things. When people come up to you and say, you have changed my life, you cough and go, oh, yeah, sure. So was I going to let me ego go rampant or remain close to the street and close to God and close to all the things I love – drugs and booze and casual violence and my girlfriend and my parents and Ireland, all the things that make being human worthwhile?'

*Shane MacGowan,* Q *(March 2000)*

'You either sit on that rocket ship and hold on for dear life or you fall off it. Yet you can't sit back and let it all go to your head. You have to keep your feet on the ground, to be careful. I've been lucky in that I haven't ever got into the drug thing, which is a big disaster for rock stars. I've only been in the business for twelve years, but I've seen them come and go. It's touched me insofar as I've seen how much damage it can do, and yes, pressure is always there and people need an escape from it, but drugs are too strong, too dangerous.'

*Dolores O'Riordan,* Cara Magazine *(March 2002)*

'"Drug" drugs are really bad for you. They can cause you an awful lot of misery. Initially, you get some great kicks, and it does give you different perspectives, and you can find all the reason in the world for taking them, but there's just as many reasons for not taking them. In fact, more. The reasons for not taking them obviously include addiction, they can change your personality without you knowin' it, so you lose control of your mind and body, and therefore you lose your dignity. And the stigma attached to taking drugs socially is bad news. A lot of people look to Keith Richards, and hold him in reverence, like a hero, but I know if Keith had his life again – he said to me – he wouldn't do them again. Sid Vicious is also held in reverence. He was just a guy fucked up on dope. It sounds like you're preachin', so I'm not even goin' to try. Just don't.'

*Phil Lynott,* Hot Press *(18 May 1984)*


'I loathed school, didn't want to be there, the pressure was getting to me and I got really sick. I went a bit mad. I took too many drugs and ended up in hospital. You know when you freak out on acid and you wake up the next morning and everything's okay? Well, one night I was still off my tits from the night before and it just didn't go away. It started in February of '95 and by September I was still fucked up. I went to psychiatrists and shrinks, all sorts. It was scary . . . I nearly died. I'm still on the rebound and . . . I don't know, I don't wanna talk about it.'

*Ash bass player Mark Hamilton,* Q *(July 1996)*

'It was a moment where I had to face a lot of things I hadn't really been facing and realise that if I was going to be able to go on and be a useful member of this band I had to beat alcohol. I had to realise that every fuck-up of mine, every problem over the last ten years that hasn't been quite so serious as that night, has been related to alcohol abuse.'

*Adam Clayton on his no-show in Sydney in December 1993,* U2: At the End of the World, *Bill Flanagan (Bantam Press 1995)*

'It was a disappointment and a wake-up call.'

*Paul McGuinness on the same topic,* U2 by U2 *(October 2006)*

'I've never liked drugs. Maybe I've never taken the good stuff, I don't know what's going on. I had some with a boyfriend once and I went completely crazy. Since I've been on the road nobody's ever offered us drugs. I think that's strange. They've never offered me any or the girls or Jim.'

*Caroline Corr,* Q *(July 1999)*

'No non-stop partying for me. I sneak away. Some very inter-esting people have been addicts and it has been associated with a certain creative freedom with some people. But the obsession with drugs in rock 'n' roll is a bit childish.'

*Cathy Davey,* Hot Press *(13 February 2008)*

'He would approach a vocal in the studio by having a joint and singing the first thing that came into his head.

Over five or six hours a song would emerge – but still only as a rough vocal. Tony Visconti, who produced the *Black Rose* album, would tear his hair out with despair, bottles of Valium and brandy under the desk. Phil was very creative, but he wouldn't always be in the right condition to work. On tour it would be a toss-up whether he could go on; he'd be sitting at the sound-check with stomach cramps. The band was a shambles and it got to the point where I couldn't face even one more gig. I left in the middle of a tour and stayed in LA for a year.'

*Gary Moore on Thin Lizzy's Phil Lynott, Q (April 1992)*

'I don't like skunk. Because I smoke a fair bit I only smoke very weak weed. I can't go for being bombed or mashed . . . I smoke daily, put it that way . . . Maybe a quarter of an ounce a week. It's a lot. If I have friends round, I cane it.'

*Sinéad O'Connor, Mojo (October 2005)*

'I've been on the edge quite a bit. I haven't not been burned, I've got close to the flame and been burned a few times, but I've fought my way out. Maybe the fact that I can talk about it now doesn't give you an idea of how it was – but I'm revealing too much here!'

*Van Morrison, Q (August 1993)*

'My first experience of drugs was as a member of a small tribe in Galway. We would collect magic mushrooms in the traditional manner, on the sacred golf course of Knock-nacarra . . . Over the next few years, some of us achieved enlightenment. Some of us died . . . A girl I liked killed herself. A girl I loved lost her mind and never found it again, and is still lost. Quite a few of us ended up in psychiatric hospitals, or with terrible depressions . . . We didn't know what we were doing, we didn't take it seriously enough. As [sci-fi writer] Philip K. Dick said of his friends, and of mine: "They wanted to have a good time, but they were like children playing in the street; they could see one after another of them being killed – run over, maimed, destroyed – but they continued to play anyhow." I have two very strong opinions on drugs. Those who are against drugs should take more of them; those who are for drugs should take less of them. Most societies make sure that their young people take dangerous drugs in controlled circumstances, very rarely, and with an experienced guide to make sure they come back with new knowledge of themselves, and of their relationship to the universe. We neck anything that's going, head down to Abrakebabra, and fight. Few achieve enlightenment in Abrakebabra.'

*Julian Gough, formerly of Toasted Heretic,* Hot Press *(13 February 2008)*

'Phil thought excess opened the channels. To become a better writer you had to live on the edge.'

*Former Thin Lizzy manager Chris O'Donnell on Thin Lizzy frontman, Phil Lynott,* Mojo *(October 2001)*

'I used to do a lot of acid when I was nineteen, twenty, and I did it for a long time, almost every day. It never fucked me up and I'm glad, because two of the friends I did it with in the squat spun off into space and never really came back. But with dope I went out of my brain for nearly a year. One night I ate hashish and tried to kill myself. I fell asleep with the radio tuned to white noise pressed against my ear. It was horrific. It freaked me out so much. That thing I tapped into inside me was so untouchably dark I never want to get into that again. So, that was it for drugs until the Seventies when the Americans began feeding us cocaine, and they supplied us with an awful lot of cocaine. That was nice for a while, up until the point where I could hear myself talking absolute bollocks and despised myself totally. And Phil Lynott slipped me a line of smack once. Horrendous. I wasn't sure whether he did it deliberately or whether it was a genuine mistake but the very minute I crawled to the toilet shaking and vomiting, he tried to get into bed with [Paula] Yates.'

*Bob Geldof,* Q *(January 1995)*


'In its simplest form, I've always seen heroin as a very evil thing. Consequently, that's always inspired a great fear of it in me, so I can assume that anyone who takes it has a similar fear. To actually have their back so much against the wall, to be controlled by it, is something I can't understand. I haven't been that close to the edge. I've certainly been near it a few times in one way or another, but to imagine that next stage is pretty much impossible.'

*Adam Clayton,* Hot Press *(March 1987)*


'It wasn't like a drink any more or a line of coke – it was getting heavier to the point where it became one long party. At the little studio round his house you couldn't work before three in the afternoon because he couldn't get himself together. I said, we could work together if you didn't fucking do this all the time. He said, yeah, you're right, I'll try to change but don't expect miracles. He meant it, but he really needed help. For Phil that would be a total admission of weakness. People would say, he's going to die, but you don't really believe it. It was quite a shock when it happened.'

*Gary Moore on collaborating with friend Phil Lynott on the hit single 'Out In The Fields', Q (April 1992)*

# ROCK 'N' ROLL

It has become such a catch-all phrase over the past few decades that rock 'n' roll' has long since lost not its original meaning (which is a euphemism for sex) but its mythic one (which is something that is rebellious or pro-vocative, or, indeed, anything that is even a shade outside the social and/or cultural norm). Yet a semblance of the attitudinal intent is apparent throughout Irish rock music; it's there in Thin Lizzy's 'Jailbreak' and 'The Boys Are Back In Town'; it's there in Rory Gallagher's plaid shirt and denims; it's there in Sinéad O'Connor's shaved head and picture-ripping; it's there in Bob Geldof's mouthings; it's there in U2's Portugese-number intro to 'Vertigo'; it's there in Divine Comedy's double entendres; it's there in the 'Drogheda – Rock City!' cry of The Golden Horde; it's there in Whipping Boy's 'Heartworm'; it's there in Glen Hansard's beard and Gavin Friday's head; it's there in My Bloody Valentine's guitars. The difference between playing it safe and playing it with a degree of challenge is all it takes to sort out the wheat from the chaff (well, hi there, Boyzone, Westlife, Ronan Keating, et al). It doesn't take much to perfect, either – just a look (preferably sly, annoyed or knowing), a laser-eyed stare, a just-so shake of the hair, a sharp word (and not just a swear word), a sigh. The truth, too. That helps.

'The possibility of infiltrating the global subconscious and deploying subliminal signposts to the metaphysical shrines of our ancestors was a fun challenge. Of course, the chance of exchanging the N7 and Tubbercurry for Route 66 and Memphis, Tennessee, proved a potent enough incentive. From the day that we released the first single, one dissenting voice could be heard: "I don't like ye since ye went heavy," it proclaimed in dressing rooms with interior decor by Attila the Hun, at windswept petrol pumps, in A&R men's offices, at chip vans whose proprietors assumed Egon Ronay to be Dr Frankenstein's assistant. Later, it would change its tune. Regularly, in fact. "I don't like ye since ye started the concepts." "I don't like ye since ye went funky." "I don't like ye since ye went acoustic." "I don't like ye since ye all went quietly mad."'

*Eamonn Carr, former Horslips drummer, recalling the glory days,* In Dublin *(3 February 1997)*

'I'm not Johnny Borrell [of Razorlight], I'm not Serge from Kasabian. I don't say outrageous things. I don't swagger. There's no "What will he say next?" with me. They probably think I'm boring. And I'm certainly not stylish. They're proper rock stars. They can back it up. They're more fun to read than me because I don't slag people off, or say we are the greatest band in the world. Are we? No, we're not. You can't walk into those shoes. They're filled by U2 and Radiohead. We aspire to be. Every day is a school day, as my dad used to say.'

*Gary Lightbody (Snow Patrol), Q (April 2007)*

'Rock 'n' roll is ridiculous. It's absurd. In the past, U2 was trying to duck that. Now, we're wrapping our arms around it and giving it a great big kiss.'

*Bono, as quoted in Mojo (December 2002)*

'Being a rock & roll star is like having a sex change! People treat you like a girl! . . . They stare at you, they follow you down the street, they hustle you. And then they try to fuck you over! It's a hard thing to talk about because it's so absurd, but actually it's valuable. When I'm with women I know what it feels like. I know what it feels like to be a babe.'

*Bono, U2: At the End of the World by Bill Flanagan (Bantam Press 1995)*

'It's very easy to see who's in this for what reasons when you see how fast they get pissed off. When I was sixteen I thought that when I was twenty I would have grown out of wanting to be in a rock 'n' roll band – your parents tell you you're going to grow out of it, everybody tells you

you're going to grow out of it and they probably hope you do as well. I'm a lot older than twenty now and I still haven't grown out of it and I know now that when I'm thirty-five I won't have stopped wanting to do this either. There's nothing else has like this. Rock 'n' roll cuts through all the shit and can appeal to an auld fella of sixty-five or a wee lad of five or six, once it's pure and true . . . it doesn't even have to be articulate. Bugger it, I'm doing this for life.'

*The 4 of Us frontman, Brendan Murphy,* Hot Press *(8 February 1990)*

'Our first musical principle was "fuck all that diddly-eyedly stuff". We were into bands like The Kinks, The Who and The Stones.'

*Bob Geldof,* The Irish Times *(October 2003)*

'Life on the road can be totally mad, I'll agree. Going to America, though, means that we can be a lot more settled. The tabloid media don't have as much a grip on us when we're away from Ireland. All they want to know about is how many drugs we're taking, or how much we drink. Sure, we're drinking, but not much more than people who go out at the weekend. Things about us are exaggerated, but in a bizarre way we don't really mind the use of shock tactics. It's funny that people actually believe it.'

*Ash drummer Rick McMurray,* In Dublin *(19 December, 1996)*

'We went over there [Hamburg] in a van, didn't even have a key for the ignition, just a screwdriver. No locks on the door either – we had to tie ropes around it. I could still see people hanging around the Star Club, like Lee Curtis & the All Stars – completely dressed in black leather. Lots of Liverpool hangover bands. Still a strong atmosphere. The Top Ten club was still going. We auditioned for it and failed – too loud!'

*Rory Gallagher, as quoted in* Mojo *(October 1998)*

'You're not allowed to grow up in rock 'n' roll.'

*Aslan's Christy Dignam,* Hot Press *(20 April 1989)*

'We didn't know what we were doing. We were six mental bohemians on a good time around Europe, more into Salvador Dali than Johnny Rotten. We never thought about having hits. Then, at twenty-five, I asked myself, what have I been doing for five years? I honestly didn't know but it had been brilliant.'

*Gavin Friday on the heady days of The Virgin Prunes,* Q *(April 1992)*

'I was very fortunate. I was paid to do something I'd have paid to do. I lived and worked with [Jimi] Hendrix. I've no regrets.'

*Eire Apparent's Ernie Graham,* Mojo *(June 1998)*

'I went out every night and stayed out all night, which was something I had never done before and haven't done

since . . . I also went off on my own, which I hadn't done before either. I found myself in all kinds of weird and wonderful situations, and though I avoided getting into serious trouble I did get into some. I had become so used to being away from home, so caught up in U2 world, the idea of coming back to any form of normality was making me nervous. I didn't know if I was ready to go back to Dublin and sleep in my own bed and get up and deal with my family and friends. Normal life looked alien to me.'
*Larry Mullen Jr on Zooropa's visit to Tokyo,* U2 by U2 *(October 2006)*

'Wake up sweaty and greasy. I don't know where the fuck I am. The phone rings. A photographer from a magazine. We have to be out in thirty minutes to be snapped somewhere. I want to die. My eyes look like a panda's, my clothes are filthy and I have to be photographed in broad daylight. Hello ladies!'
*Therapy?'s Andy Cairns,* Q *(August 1995)*

'What do you plan to do after the tour ends? Extend the tour . . . reality isn't what it's cracked up to be.'
*Bono,* Zoo TV *Tour Programme (1992)*

'It was kinda frightening when you saw Hamburg the first time . . . It's just as well we didn't know how dangerous it was! But it was a great starting ground, plus you were more or less allowed to play what you wanted. But you had long sets to play – you'd play forty-five minutes of the hour for six sets a night, which wasn't that tough compared to some of the bands that used have to do eight or nine sets ... You'd get fine blisters in your left hand from that and sore throats.'

*Rory Gallagher in conversation with Colm Keane, RTÉ 1 (30 August 1985)*

'On the road, you enter this twilight zone, this other reality, and you get home and all this time's gone by. For you it seems like you just left. For everyone else, all this stuff's been happening. You do lose a chunk of your life. But there's other massive compensations. We're very lucky, we have the opportunity to bring our friends and family out from time to time ... So it's not like it used to be in the early days when you'd go on the road and you literally wouldn't see anyone for two or three months. That was more difficult. But then, that was about survival. This isn't really about survival – this is about doing great work.'

*Edge,* Mojo *(July 2005)*

'They [Ireland's 1980's rock 'n' roll brotherhood] were so hard to work with. They had to have road crew, they wanted riders [comfort zone accessories such as food, drink, bowls of white-only smarties, etc] and they'd only play their own music. Nobody wanted to know about bands doing their own music – they wanted to hear something they'd recognise, so that just didn't work. Perhaps one or two songs that were being played on the radio would go down well, but the rest of the night people were bored. The places these rock bands would play were basic ballrooms – a stage, a dressing room, and a place to take the money. So I hated doing that, it wasn't really my thing at all. I didn't like the bands, the attitude, the music, the way some of them acted like stars when we all knew a number of them hyped their records into the charts. I only did it for the money – I had to make a living. I was just about able to pay my phone bills and my rent.'

*Pop impresario Louis Walsh,* Cara Magazine *(July 2002)*

'Death to whingeing rock stars, their miserable entourages and their ten bodyguards. I never needed a security guy. I had one on the road once because there were some death threats at the time and he was taking his job seriously, but I used to sneak away from him, get offside . . . You go out onto the streets of Chicago with two giants and people are gonna start paying attention. I avoid that stuff and as a result I have much more fun than your regular rock star.'

*Bono,* Q *(February 2002)*

'Phillip [Lynott] was in love with the idea of rock 'n' roll. I've no time for his idea of what rock 'n' roll is all about. Part of him knew it was a load of bollocks but part of him also believed it to be true. Like, I remember he called me just before we went to a premiere or something and I said "We'll get cab". He said "Are you fuckin' kiddin', man. We gotta get a limo!" For Philip, rock 'n' roll was very much a way out. From fifteen, he believed that, but it was never for me . . . I could have done other things. Philip was a great guy, so full of the life-force, he'd fill you with it. But he also was desperately in love with the rock 'n' roll dream. I'm not. He loved it and truly believed it was a valid way to live . . . And die, absolutely.'

*Bob Geldof,* Hot Press *(December 1989)*

'It suits us that people believe we're choirboys, 'cos it means we can get away with murder.'

*Larry Mullen Jr,* Mojo *(July 2005)*

'The Outcasts leave no lasting musical heritage. Our best songs were recorded when we couldn't play well enough to do them justice, but then we weren't making music to be analysed years later, it was all about now, throwing out all that went before and having our moment in the spotlight. My favourite review is one in *NME* that said even before we started to play, we looked and moved like a real band! I'm especially proud none of us even talked about re-forming, there is no sadder sight than four fat balding middle-aged men singing about being teenage rebels, but it was a magical time to be young when with three chords and a killer haircut you could be a rock star.'

*The Outcasts' Greg Cowan,* It Makes You Want To Spit *(Reekus Music 2003)*

'I'm a dedicated rock 'n' roller. There are times when I think we might be going too far – and I definitely worry about Rick [McMurray, drummer] because he's really close to becoming an alcoholic – but then I just go, fuck it, I

don't care, I'm going out and I'm going to get fucked up.'
*Ash bass player Mark Hamilton,* Q *(July 1996)*

'It was kind of weird going back to houses at night because there was no room service. I preferred staying in hotels.'
*Adam Clayton on the band decamping nightly to the Hamptons during the* Rattle And Hum *tour,* U2 by U2 *(October 2006)*

'If you do a million gigs you've lots of funny incidents. Some you can retell and some you can't . . . All the standard things like falling off stage and electric shocks and all the usual practical jokes that go on. But the scariest one, I think, was in Italy. I just ran over to the side of the stage during the show playing a guitar break and I didn't realise there was a big open black trap door without the door in it, you know. And the next thing I was falling into this void. Through some miracle I put my hands up in the air and there was a kind of a bar sticking out of the side of the wall, and I grabbed on to it, so I was swinging Tarzan-fashion . . . The audience thought this was part of the act or something, so I just swung back on to the stage and hit the right note and ploughed away . . . Some places you play, you don't get a chance to see where the floorboards are . . .'
*Rory Gallagher in conversation with Colm Keane, RTÉ 1 (30 August 1985)*

'I used to get up late because I stayed up late because I worked late. Now, I discovered I really like to see the sun come up and that's when I do my reading and writing, and now it's when I drop my kids to school. It's not very rock 'n' roll, but it's very rock 'n' roll.'

*Bono,* Irish Mail on Sunday *(24 February 2008)*

'I'm sure I've been a nasty piece of work now and again – I'm only human, after all – but I'd like to pride myself that I'm always aware of how quite ridiculous you look when you act like Johnny Rock Star. It can only backfire, and when it backfires you will most certainly be reminded that it was not a good idea to wear those pair of silver leather trousers.'

*Therapy? singer Andy Cairns,* The Irish Times *(June 2006)*

'He was a dandy. He turned heads. It was central to his charisma. He grasped it and ran with it. He was the first Dublin guy to realise being a rock star had to do with defining and perfecting an image.'

*Television director/producer Dave Heffernan on Thin Lizzy's Phil Lynott,* Mojo *(December 1993)*

# RELIGION

We are what we are, and you can't take it away from us whether you want to or not. Religion is ingrained for most, with religious teachings scored into the psyche, our attitudes towards the religious hierarchies informed initially by the role model figures of school days, latterly by the drastic about-face of public acceptance for sections of the (notably) Catholic priesthood and hierarchy. In the area of rock 'n' roll, religion, frankly, can't compete let alone win. U2 are, possibly, the only Irish rock band (indeed, for a band of their stature, quite likely the only rock band per se) to have openly – to their credit, without fear of cynicism or reprisal – espoused religious/spiritual elements in their music, and for them it seems to remain something of a touchstone, a constant. U2, however, come across as discerning, questioning spiritually motivated people – they engage with the subject, they appear to know the subject, and they are unabashed in admitting that the Bible forms part of their lyrical inspiration. Other Irish acts are not so upfront; Van Morrison touches on certain, perhaps metaphysical elements in his generally woeful music, but it's so abstract it's virtually impossible to grasp it. Sinéad O'Connor actually became a priest (for a brief spell), but gradually flitted from that to becoming immersed in the ganja smoke (and mirrors) of Rastafarianism. Some people, meanwhile, see God at the point of orgasm. That'd be Andrea Corr, then.

'I think that certain people act in the name of religion, but they have little to do with its central message. For instance, those who murder in the name of Islam have profoundly misunderstood its message of peace and love. For Osama Bin Laden to say he represents Islam is as wrong and disgusting as people like the IRA saying that they speak for Catholics. There will always be a minority of assholes who are determined to get hold of the wrong end of the stick. But the finger shouldn't just be pointed at Islam. There is similar stuff in the Jewish and Christian scriptures. But I ignore those bits. It's the peaceful and loving sections that inspire me.'

*Sinéad O'Connor,* Uncut *(July 2007)*

'As I get older I get more religious . . . because I'm goin' to die fuckin' soon. The odds are more in God's favour . . . Once you're Irish and Catholic, you're always Irish and Catholic. I think it's in you. You can never disassociate yourself from it. You can acquire another accent, but it'll always be there in your head. The rules that were beaten into me at schoool are ingrained. I still know when I commit a mortal or a venial sin, y'know? My definition of a good Catholic? A man who lives by his own conscience, but has enough perspective on his conscience to make sure it doesn't get corrupted. It is so easy to corrupt your conscience . . . The first time you take some sherry out of the cabinet and you replace what you've taken with water, and you think, "I didn't get caught". You do it again, until one day, the bottle is all water, so you have to get caught. That's the way your conscience can get corrupted.'

*Phil Lynott,* Hot Press *(18 May 1984)*

'He [Van Morrison] asked me a lot of questions . . . Once I was having a meal with him, and he said to me – it was almost his first question – he said, "What do you think about the blood of Jesus?" It's a strange question for a rock musician to ask.'

Too Late To Stop Now *by Steve Turner (Bloomsbury 1993)*

'The showband/dancehall explosion of the 1960s and 1970s was the most radical and effective force in the breaking of the conservative monolith of post-Famine Irish Catholicism, which, by losing touch with human reality had reduced religion to a form of policing.'

*John Waters,* The Irish Times *(January 2008)*

'About ten years ago, every Sunday morning, the man in the flat below me used to tune his radio to Mass, a ceremony much loved by Catholics in Ireland, but fuckin' dreadful if it comes at you through plaster and floorboards from a bad radio – and you're an atheist with a hangover.

# Religion

I used to put on 'Never Mind the Bollocks' . . . but I don't know if he ever noticed. I never asked him.'
*Writer Roddy Doyle,* Mojo *(August 1997)*

'I haven't been to church since I was eighteen. I used to fall asleep or I used to play the church organ and I sat in the back playing Nik Kershaw with the organ turned down really low . . . The priest is yapping away and I'd be rocking out in the corner.'
*Dolores O'Riordan,* Q *(May 1996)*

'Permanent holy hour and muzak.'
*Rory Gallagher's concept of Hell,* Hot Press *(22 July 1983)*

'I'm a materialist. I don't believe in anything paranormal . . . I have no time for church, and this born-again Christian thing to me is ludicrous . . . Christianity gets a lot of its followers from people who are really down – who are literally willing to go down on their knees for God to help them. It's sad, and I think this particular ideology is unhealthy in music, appealing to people's desperation. But I don't feel that way about U2. They're very good at what they do and have great power live. It's a raw kind of power that can't be manufactured . . . To the extent that Bono's a Christian, well I must give him his due: he's gotten involved in a lot of worthwhile things – the anti-apartheid movement and the Hiroshima thing. Self Aid? I think it's dangerous to fuck around with something as serious as unemployment on an abstract, Christian level.'
*Paul Cleary, formerly of The Blades,* Hot Press *(5 June 1986)*

# Rockaganda

'Fight the real enemy.'

*Sinéad O'Connor rips apart a photograph of Pope John Paul II, US television show* Saturday Night Live *(3 October 1992)*

'My religious sense doesn't come from the Church, it comes from music ... gospel music. It's a much more universal spirituality ... I did some research on religion by myself. If my family had been very religious, I doubt whether it would have interested me. I'm more likely to reject things which people try to impose on me. When I was young in Belfast, I saw so many Catholics and Protestants for whom religion was a burden. There was enormous pressure and you had to belong to one or the other community. Thank God my parents were strong enough not to give in to this pressure.'

*Van Morrison, as quoted in* Can You Feel The Silence? A New Biography of Van Morrison *by Clinton Heylin (Viking Books 2002)*

'I can remember being seven years old and being told "you're going to burn in a lake of fire for all eternity." And there you're sitting there thinking, Christ!'

*Andy Cairns, Therapy?, Q (March 1994)*

'I don't have any religion. I don't have anything to do with the Catholic Church at all – except sometimes in my work, or in my day-to-day living, when I would meet priests or I would meet nuns and would get on perfectly well with them ... I take people as I find them. But I don't believe in the Catholic Church. I drifted away from it

when I was about seventeen or eighteen when I was in the bank . . . more from laziness, really. I stopped goin' to mass. But it's only in the last seven years or so, when I started to examine things a bit more closely, that I would have actually come to say that I have absolutely no religion whatsoever now. Or I wouldn't accept anything from the Catholic Church.'
*Christy Moore,* Hot Press *(15 June 1984)*

'The Undertones – they're a Protestant band.'
*Said to* Hot Press *writer, Bill Graham, on a visit to Derry,* Hot Press *(18 August 1983)*

'I want to make it clear that I never did support the IRA. I was entirely under the influence of a fifty-year-old man who I was in love with. And I would parrot all his views. I don't regret saying that because I feel that it wasn't me saying it, I was just a young woman in awe and in love. I didn't have any identity of my own. When I finally understood what the fuck it was I was saying, I felt sick with myself.'
*Sinéad O'Connor,* Uncut *(July 2007)*

'I think God is a gas character. If he's out there he must be a very funny man!'
*Something Happens frontman, Tom Dunne,* Hot Press *(28 June 1990)*

'Wouldn't it be great just to be born and nobody told you that there was such a thing called religion? Say it didn't exist and you were just told that all you've got is this life and that's it, you know. There's no heaven, no hell. Most people at this point question religion . . . I certainly do, and I think a lot of people question religion because it hasn't really done the human race that much good, has it?'

*Van Morrison,* Mojo *(August 1995)*

'The church has nothing to do with God . . . It's just an industry, it's a money-making organization. Besides, obviously it's not working . . .'

*Sinéad O'Connor,* Hot Press *(12 December 1991)*

# POLITICS

It's a hoary old cliché − should rock musicians and/or people involved in entertaining the population at large be brave or foolhardy (or, indeed, knowledgeable) enough to speak out on various political matters? We'll leave world affairs (rainforests, Africa, G8, carbon footprinting, etc) for another time, perhaps, and just focus on Irish ways and Irish laws. Certainly, there are people passionate enough to offer thought-provoking opinions on localised issues such as the 'Troubles' and associated component parties such as the IRA. There are also people who, in the fervid innocence of youth, admit to having shot their mouths off only to regret it years later. The truth is, politics is an adult game played for the most part by people who have little or no genuine emotionally reflexive responses to rock music. You'll be glad to hear that this doesn't make them bad people, just people who don't get the nuances of the rock-star lifestyle. Similarly, the 'entertainers'/'celebrities' who, by and large, don't have access to the inner workings of the Cabinet don't fully understand the machinations of the political process. Where passion and politics intersect, however, is where sparks fly. Safety goggles at the ready!

'Cliff Moore, owner of IT Records, with retails outlets in Portadown, Lurgan, Banbridge and Lisburn, went to London in the summer of '77 to purchase some punk records. He paid a visit to several of the independent labels including Chiswick Records, who were based in an office above the Rock On record shop. Inspired by the chaos and enthusiasm that he encountered at Chiswick, Cliff returned home and decided to start his own label. Simply called IT Records, Cliff ran the new label from his shop at 8 Thomas Street, Portadown . . . Sadly, all files and data relating to the label, and Cliff's own spare copies of the singles, were destroyed when an IRA car bomb devastated his shop in an explosion in Portadown town centre.'

It Makes You Want To Spit *(Reekus Music 2003)*

JW: 'Do you support the Provisionals?'

CM: 'Yes.'

JW: 'Do you know any IRA volunteers personally?'

CM: 'Oh God yeah. I've been in the H-Blocks, on visits. I know an awful lot of volunteers. I know much more IRA volunteers than I know Special Branch men! . . . I find [volunteers] to be quite amazing, actually. I find it very hard to imagine the attitude I had towards the IRA volunteers, ten years ago, with the knowledge I have of the IRA volunteers I know now, and the kind of people they are, and the sacrifices they make, and the lives they lead.'

# Politics

JW: 'What attitudes did you have?'

CM: 'About ten years ago, I belonged to the body of people who believed that the IRA controlled all the vice and all the . . . y'know? I believed everything I read in the *Sunday World* and the *Hot Press*, before I tried to find out for myself.'

JM: 'What do you say to people who say that in your music you incite people to hatred and bigotry and violence?'

CM: 'Well, the position which I have now towards the Republican Movement is one which has grown within me over the last seven or eight years, as a result of what I've experienced myself in the Six Counties, as a result of what I've seen and as a result of what I know to be true. So, as far as I'm concerned, my position and my music have come about as a direct result of personal experience. I would never incite people to bigotry. But I do react to the bigotry which I myself have experienced. And despite what the *Hot Press* might print, or what the media might print, I don't consider the Republican Movement to be a bigoted organisation. I *do* consider the UDR and the RUC to be full of bigotry.'

*Excerpt from interview with Christy Moore by John Waters,* Hot Press *(15 June 1984)*

'That Self Aid was motivated by compassionate idealism in its inception can be taken as read. That its ideals went unrealised is, in retrospect, probably the most charitable thing that can be said about the whole concept. Be kind, and bear in mind it was the mid-'80s. Much in the same way as Rubik's Cubes, the New Romantics and mullet hairstyles, Self Aid was a product of its time. It was the Age of the Bunfight, and if Bob Geldof's Live Aid was the Daddy of them all, Red Wedge was the rebellious daughter's militant rantings and USA For Africa was the son who developed Yuppie tendencies, turned self-promotional and got all flash, (then) Self Aid was the Crusty of the family who went on the doss, had his dog on a string and never really amounted to anything,'

*Ian O'Doherty,* In Dublin *(3 February 1997)*

'The politics in Ireland doesn't reflect what's going on with the people. It's shocking really that the country hasn't produced a politician with a sense of anger, or a sense of newness. All the politicians look like your older distant relative.'

*Morrissey,* The Irish Times *(November 1999)*

'I was very young and I didn't know what I was talking about. Obviously, one has compassion and understanding for the circumstances that drive people to violence. But, y'know, especially for someone like me who'd come from violence, to talk like that was bollocks.'

*Sinéad O'Connor on her pro-IRA statements she had made early on in her career,* Mojo *(October 2005)*

'To me, with That Petrol Emotion, the whole thing about Northern Ireland has become very trendy. But y'see, they

don't consider that people have to live through it. Like, I read last week that [US singer] Michelle Shocked is trying to get speeches by IRA men on the radio . . . That's all great if you're an American and you can say it from there, but what about somebody who lives here . . . What about the other people, the real people it matters to.'
*Stiff Little Fingers' Henry Cluney,* Hot Press *(20 April 1989)*

'That Petrol Emotion were a really underrated band. I can still hear John Peel's voice introducing one of their sessions. They were really politicised and did these great press releases to try to change people's perception of Northern Ireland.'
*Manic Street Preachers' Nicky Wire,* Q *(February 2008)*

'The way Belfast is set out, there's a lot of areas where . . . if we were a band living in the Falls Road or the Shankill, we'd have to be careful about what we were singing or writing about, whereas around this area here [near Queen's University] there's people from all over the city who mix and exchange views. It's about the only area of Belfast where there is a near-normal environment.'
*Bernard, of Big Self,* Hot Press *(15 October 1981)*

'As a consequence of . . . provincialism, showbands and dancehalls are in popular cultural memory analogous to the Civil War in our political neurology. Though patently central to the social and cultural story, they have fallen foul of a self-induced amnesia, rendered unmentionable by virtue of being deemed incompatible with modern aspirations. This makes for bad history and confused identity . . . To attempt a genealogy of the latter-day generation of Irish pop superstars without acknowledging the showbands is like discussing Irish politics without mentioning de Valera. It can be done but it sounds mad.'

*John Waters,* The Irish Times *(January 2008)*

'Fulfilling the basic criteria of the showband days there were seven of them . . . so at least the punters could kid themselves that they were somehow getting value for money, but by Christ what a racket they made. Uilleann pipes, bouzoukis, saxophones, electric guitars, bodhrans and the dreaded fretless bass all clattering along and trying not to bump into each other, with the whole cacophonous caboodle topped off by Christy Moore's completely out-of-context vocals and a political stance pitched – without any sense of irony, these were folkies remember – somewhere between Amnesty International, CND and an *An Phoblacht* editorial. No benefit gigs in East Belfast for these lads.'

*From 'The Worst Dublin Bands In The World . . . Ever' series, by George Byrne,* In Dublin *(29 August 1996)*

'There's grief and there's grief. People lost their lives and suffered terribly. I had nuisance, but no grief, not the way they felt it during the huger strikes. That's grief. Warrington . . . that's grief. All I had was bits of nuisance, being held up at places . . . minor consequences not worthy of mention. Other people lost their lives. There've been times when I was afraid, yes. Frightened? Definitely. Such as? I've been in frightening situations and I've been scared, that's all I'll say . . . In the north and south and in the UK I had experiences I could have done without but I'm still not going to say I suffered. I didn't get beaten up or banged up or kicked or knee-capped . . . Listen, I have nothing bad to say about England. Nothing.'

*Christy Moore,* Mojo *(May 2006)*

'I made a conscious decision to leave there, two years ago. Regardless of what happened I don't think I'd return to Derry. I've been to other places and seen how other people live. I've a taste for it and I crave for a little more of it. Besides, it now boils down to the fact that I've got an eighteen-month old son and there's shit-all there for him. And even on that level, I do not intend to raise my family in Northern Ireland, at this moment.'

*Feargal Sharkey, formerly of The Undertones,* Hot Press *(18 August 1983)*

'What I grew up in was this cosy de Valera consensus of Church and State. And The Boomtown Rats coming into being was a rejection of that consensus. I do believe we were among the first to post these Lutheran ideas on the church door. We were saying back then: "this is no longer going to be where's it at." And I think our songs grasped at an understanding of that, certainly 'Banana Republic' did. I look at the tribunals taking place now and I hope they are the end process of what we helped to begin – that could be our legacy. And all this bollocks about the Celtic Tiger – I'll tell you who the real tigers are, it's the men and women who came to Britain in the 1950s and kept the country afloat sending money back home. You see them now in London, no social insurance, no pensions – these helpless, deracinated people. We've abandoned them and it's wrong. They sent back their wages to us. These are the people who gave us Morrissey and The Smiths, who gave us Johnny Rotten, Elvis Costello, Oasis.'

*Bob Geldof,* The Irish Times *(October 2003)*

'Moving Hearts are not a proposition unanimously approved by all in the rock community. They set up issues, compel responses. Controversies of politics and culture are unavoidable with Moving Hearts. Moving Hearts, with Christy Moore in the van, vigorously supported the H–Block cause, a position that definitely disaffected the Northern rock contingent and more at both the Castlebar and Lisdoonvarna festivals, a nervousness best expressed by one Belfast-ite who feared the consequences should Moving Hearts be booked into the college that person controlled. No Irish band has ever been so explicit in its support of a political cause, and that an issue that particularly unsettles the Irish rock community. The relationship between Irish rock and politics aren't as simple as in Britain. There exists a consensus that Ronald Reagan, Margaret Thatcher, unemployment and the bomb are bad but in Ireland — it is the equivalent unemployed who kill and maim each other. Of necessity, Irish rock has striven to escape into a non-sectarian space, even at the cost of being apolitical. It is no accident that the North's first fanzine should be called *Alternative Ulster*, nor that its founders, Gavin Martin and Dave McCullough, in their later careers at *NME* and *Sounds* should be more sceptical than their companions about British efforts to mate music and radical politics.'

*Bill Graham,* Hot Press *(30 October 1981)*

'People were afraid to come to Northern Ireland, apart from Rory Gallagher who came every year, but generally British bands were obviously either frightened to come across, ignorant or couldn't get the insurance. Realistically, [Belfast] wasn't the nicest place to go to: they had security gates around the city centre that were locked around eight o'clock in the evening, which made the city centre a ghost town.'

*Stiff Little Fingers frontman Jake Burns,* State *(April 2008)*

'I got letters from various representatives of Sinn Féin to tell me that I wasn't to discuss those things. And so I told them to fuck themselves. If you're gonna tell the Grammys to shove it up your arse . . . then you have to tell Sinn Féin to shove it up their arse as well.'

*Sinéad O'Connor on her promise to talk about punishment beatings,* Mojo *(October 2005)*


'Okay, Punk Rockering up and down in France or England was one thing, but getting to Ulster was another. Although having the first concert cancelled was a big disappointment for everyone, at least it allowed for some close band/audience contact. If Punk was hard, Ulster was harder. If Punk was chaos, Ulster was "war zone". Punk was the perfect soundtrack to the ravaged cities. Outside the Ulster Hall, in the melee, punks were lying down in the street in front of the Land Rover patrols and armoured cars. After the crowd was dispersed we went on a spree with the local crew and got a rapid education in the ways of the province. The punks informed us they were the only integrated peoples in the whole country. Let the child teach the man! Although there was a good twelve months before the mighty [Stiff Little] Fingers and The Undertones began to rise, you could tell something was coming from just looking at the fans. They were bursting with energy and enthusiasm, not at all cowed by the special difficulties of the place and beyond all reach of bigoted tradition. Seasons come and go and the music is constantly changing, but when punk rock ruled over Ulster nobody ever had more excitement and fun. Between the bombings and shootings, the religious hatred and the settling of old scores, punk gave everybody a chance to LIVE for one glorious burning moment.'

*Joe Strummer,* It Makes You Want To Spit *(Reekus Music 2003)*

'We got torn to pieces by The Undertones ... who should have known better because they lived through it. And as soon as they split up, the first thing the O'Neill brothers do is start writing political songs about Northern Ireland. I fell about laughing when I saw that. I'm not having a go at them, I think it's great that they've finally decided that's what they want to do. But really, the people that slagged us off either didn't know what was happening, or else did and chose to bury their heads in the sand like so many people up there do.'

*Stiff Little Fingers member Jake Burns responding to the accusation that in singing about Northern Irish politics they were exploiting the misery and suffering involved,* Hot Press *(11 February 1988)*

# COURTS OF LAW

Where there is rock 'n' roll, there is trouble, and where there is trouble there is the law, and where there is the law, there is a court. Funnily enough, the instances of Irish rock stars being in court are few and far between; there was the case some years ago of Bono looking for his trousers back from former U2 stylist Lola Cashman; there have been various litigious cases over the years between certain members of Irish rock bands and their employees, between certain members of Irish rock bands and their managers, and between certain members of Irish rock bands and their colleagues. There have, of course, been occasional altercations with the police involving soft drugs (come on down, Adam Clayton!), as well as flurries of solicitor–client activity, but by and large it seems that Irish rockers are a genteel lot, prone, perhaps, to bouts of anti-authoritarianism and too much a liking for beer, but generally too decent a bunch to annoy the boys in blue. Mind you, those Westlife chaps – keep your eye on them; you never know what they might get up to.

❖

'We had a deal going with the guy in the school tuck shop. He'd give us two or three quids' worth of sweets and a fiver in change every day. We were so bad! Over the course of a year more than a grand went missing, and it was a really big deal, the police were called in and everything! We had to deny all knowledge. If our old headmaster reads this he'll have us in court next week. He's still upset about it.'

*Ash's Mark Hamilton,* Q *(July 1996)*

'Barely had I enlisted a research assistant to start making calls, when a solicitor was calling her up, professing to represent Mr Morrison and uttering the immortal phrase "This is not a threatening phone call, but . . ."'

*From the preface to Clinton Heylin's biography of Van Morrison,* Can You Feel The Silence? *(Viking Books 2002)*

'When it came to [Van] Morrison's attention that Ms [Linda Gail] Lewis had been interviewed for this very book, a letter from his Belfast solicitors was sent to a number of the larger British book distributors, asserting that the (as yet unfinished, sight unseen) biography contained "a number of false allegations of an extremely serious defamatory nature" that was alleged to emanate from Ms Lewis. When at least four newspapers published comments by Lewis about her time with Morrison, they found themselves on the receiving end of writs for libel.'

*Clinton Heylin's biography of Van Morrison,* Can You Feel The Silence? *(Viking Books 2002)*

# Rockaganda

'The band also visited America with The Animals, then with Hendrix and Soft Machine, but catastrophe struck when [Henry] McCullough was arrested for marijuana possession. Ernie Graham remembers the incident blithely: "Henry had the knack of mixing with shady characters. I'd warned him: don't involve me. But he had people in our room, smoking dope, and I got back and found three policemen there. I was held overnight, before Henry gave a statement I wasn't involved and I was released. But for the rest of the tour, every time I heard footsteps I imagined people coming to arrest me."'

*Eire Apparent's brush with the law, as told to writer Trevor Hodgett, Mojo (June 1998)*

'I am a celebrity in this country . . . I don't have the time to talk . . . You will do yourself a lot of harm as I am well known high-up . . . Stop messing . . . You'll be sorry for this . . . I am the bass player with U2 and I want to go to bed.'

*A selection of conversational snippets from Adam Clayton to Garda Gerard Walsh on the evening of 2 March 1984. [Clayton drove through a Garda checkpoint, subsequently dragging Garda Walsh along the road for over forty feet when Walsh had reached in to Clayton's car to switch off the ignition. Clayton thereafter pleaded guilty to dangerous driving and driving with excess alcohol. He was disqualified from driving for two years.* Gubu Nation *by Damian Corless (2004)*

# WORDS/MUSIC

It is the bedrock, the foundation, the inherent worth. If the music doesn't get you, then the words will, and vice versa. Sometimes, the melody lines come out of the blue, the words out of thin air. Sometimes, on waking up of a morning after the night before, the song is virtually fully formed and needs only a sprucing up in the recording studio before going on to make the songwriter more money than you will ever see in your life. While certain people term this songwriting, others call it either divine intervention or jammy-bastard luck. Whatever way it is viewed, the end result is what is most important: is the song fab or not? Does it say something to the listener other than the obvious lyrical content? Does the music transport the listener outside the realm of basic day-to-day life? Musicians, we reckon, are some of the most creative, luckiest people in the world, but they are hidebound to success and must, we also reckon, be under immense pressure to come up with the goods again and again. Otherwise, they end up being remembered for that one truly brilliant song (or album) of God-knows-how-many years ago, and a rake of not-so good material ever since. Are we sorry for them? Er, no, not really.

'I like it when I manage to transport my thinking brain to somewhere else, just let fly. And it's my lifeline. It's the reason why I can feed my kids and why I didn't have to marry some millionaire with a tiny dick. It is my soul in lots of way. It's the time I most feel like me.'
*Sinéad O'Connor on her singing voice,* Mojo *(October 2005)*

'I really do get lost for long periods of time – it would probably drive other people mad, melodies day and night. They're always in my head; everything else is irrelevant. I don't even listen to other music, none at all.'
*Enya,* Hot Press *(27 July 1989)*

'Of course there are parallels, and it would be naive of me to say that it was a blind coincidence!'
*Gavin Friday on U2 being occasionally influenced by him,* Mojo *(March 1996)*

'I can't relate to that at all.'
*Van Morrison on being asked is it important that his music is listened to in 100 years time,* Uncut *(July 2005)*

'I'm bitter! I'm twisted! James Joyce is fucking my sister!'
*One of Irish rock's weirdest lyrics, courtesy of Therapy?'s Andy Cairns' song, 'Potato Junkie'.*

'[U2's] lyrics don't particularly appeal to me – I suppose they might appeal to a 16- or 17-year-old looking for something vaguely spiritual, tired of consumerism, and McDonalds burgers, looking for something better.'

*Paul Cleary,* Hot Press *(June 5 1986)*

'I was told by every record company in London who would listen that 'Teenage Kicks' by The Undertones was crap. I remember touting the record to CBS in London and being forcibly ejected from their offices. The night, after I had come home, I was listening to John Peel, who was playing a copy which I had left in the BBC for him. When it finished, he said "Wasn't that the most wonderful record you ever heard in the world?" and played it again, the first time ever that he had played a record twice in his show.'

*Terri Hooley,* It Makes You Want To Spit *(Reekus Music 2003)*

'Sometimes, I feel I should sit down and write the record that totally sums up what I'm trying to do. I can't wait forever to make that type of record. I've made oddball record after oddball record, and there are some great moments on them and I like the whole feel of them, but . . . the essence of me, whether some people agree or disagree, is not to make po-faced albums. Sometimes I try to be dumb on purpose, which may be even worse. My publisher says that I'm like a old fashioned pop songwriter – intelligence within three-to-four minutes. And that *is* what I try to do – not to be intelligent for its own sake, but to have something more than a beat and a hook that you can't get out of your brain.'

*Neil Hannon (Divine Comedy),* Cara Magazine *(June 2003)*

'The one [record] that made me want to be involved in music was 'Daydream Nation' by Sonic Youth. I went to see them when I was 14 in Manchester and I came away a different person. They were so brilliant. The next day I sold all my U2 records and bought it.'

*Róisín Murphy (formerly of Moloko),* Mojo *(November 2007)*

'I have a policy about writing songs – I can't force myself to write one, and I try to make a conscious decision not to look at it too closely and overwrite it. Some people try to pick apart what they do, and I think the most interesting things about my writing and other people's writings are the cracks or the bits in yourself that you don't think too hard about. Sometimes, it's the bits you don't think about that work.'

*Fat Lady Sings' Nick Kelly,* Hot Press *(30 November 1989)*

'Looking back, there's no way we were ready. But it was punk rock and you struck when the iron was hot and got on with it. When you listen back to that first single now, it's incredibly naive, it's incredibly badly played and hardly produced at all.'

*Stiff Little Fingers frontman Jake Burns on 'Suspect Device',* State *(April 2008)*

'It's the words, though – full of cheap emotions, teeth-clenching rhymes, doubtful moralizing and tired metaphors – where you tend to throw the towel in. It does, though, take a genius of sorts to condense a couple of hundred years of medieval history into eight and a bit minutes of song, and Chris de Burgh takes up the challenge on *Crusader* without so much as a blush.'

*Excerpt from review of Chris de Burgh re-issues,* Q *(July 1995)*

'[I remember] listening to washing machines and engines of cars and I'd hear sentences, you know, then string them all together . . . We have an upright piano, and I'd come home after being out on the town and sit under the keyboard and write. Three of the songs on the album [*Who Do You Think I Am?*] all came in one night . . . The songs exist apart from me. They're floating around and I catch them.'

*Sinéad Lohan,* Mojo *(February 1996)*

'The word "macho" has really become associated with chauvinist. You always see "male chauvinist". For some reason there doesn't seem to be female chauvinist at all . . . I seem to get that a lot. Now, I do write about masculine things. Joni Mitchell writes about feminine things. For me, I get a great insight as to how females think, from her songs. What I was tryin' to do – these are the Lizzy songs – I was just givin' a masculine point of view, talkin' about my own aggression – which obviously might cross over into the chauvinist thing. Not knowin' me father, and always bein' surrounded by women – wife, daughter, mother ... – I've always enjoyed female company. I'd hate to think that anybody who knew me to that extent would think that I'm chauvinist.'

*Phil Lynott,* Hot Press *(18 May 1984)*

'Van Morrison is interested, *obsessed* with how much musical or verbal information he can compress into a small space, and almost conversely, how far he can spread one note, word, sound or picture. To capture one moment, be it a caress or a twitch. He repeats certain phrases to extremes that from anybody else would seem ridiculous, because he's waiting for a vision to unfold, trying as unobtrusively as possible to nudge it along. Sometimes he gives it to you through silence, by choking off the song in mid–flight.'

*Lester Bangs,* Psychotic Reactions and Carburetor Dung *(William Heinemann 1988)*

'The Pogues got Irish music by the scruff of the neck and just ripped it up. They weren't confined by any law and they didn't belong to any country or to any hierarchy, so they were really shocking to some of the traditional Irish musicians. They reacted to The Pogues the way people had originally reacted to the Sex Pistols.'

*The Pogues' one-time manager Frank Murray,* Mojo *(September 2004)*

'I only write what I have to write about, because I feel it strongly enough. It's not that I wake up in the morning and go, "I have to write this". I'm not driven in that sense, because I'm as lazy as the next man. When I write a song, and get a sense of an emotion that is strong, I know I'll get a good song out of it. I've always felt that one of the most exciting things that human beings can do is to make a relationship develop. Some people use politics to do that. For me, where it's really white hot is in the one-to-one situation. I would not feel great about myself if I couldn't make a fundamental relationship work with another human being. This, in fact, is not simply a question of the romantic or sexual – it could be a friend-ship. I've had lots of friendships in my life that have gone wrong, and it always leaves you with a sense of loss and failure even though it may not be your fault. But to me, friendships and relationships are the be-all and end-all of being human. It's exciting and difficult to make it work. It's what motivates me in terms of a broad philosophy, so it's natural I would want to write about my successes and failures in that.'

*Paul Brady,* Cara Magazine *(November 1999)*

'The way U2 works is maybe like a painter in that we don't have a structure, we just start to improvise and discover the song whilst singing it.'

*Bono,* Mojo *(April 2002)*

'Maybe I should write a new song called "I Did More Than Summer In Dublin"...We recorded over thirty-five songs and yet to most people we will always be "Summer In Dublin", "Leeson Street Lady" and "Rock 'n' Roll

Fantasy". These are not my favourites among our songs. It got to a stage where I couldn't even enjoy doing them on stage. And when you reach that point you shouldn't be up there.'

*Bagatelle's Liam Reilly,* Hot Press *(11 August 1988)*

'Find a song that will support people who I perceive are repressed and need my support, then I am glad to do it. If I can't write a song about it I will bring a song I already know into it . . . Songs do have the power to change things. Music has changed my life . . . it has changed everyone's lives.'

*Christy Moore,* Mojo *(May 2006)*

'It can't be another batch of songs about screwing things up and being sorry, I just can't live like that. This one'll just have to be about celibacy and wanking.'

*Gary Lightbody (Snow Patrol) on forthcoming album,* Eyes Open, Q *(August 2004)*

'Kirsty knew exactly the right measure of viciousness and femininity and romance to put into it and she had a very strong character, and it came across in a big way. The guy in the song is any drunken waster bastard, that's what I represent on that record . . . In operas, if you have a double aria, it's what the woman does that really matters. The man lies, the woman tells the truth.'

*Shane MacGowan on 'Fairytale Of New York',* Mojo *(September 2004)*

'The problem with the Wolfe Tones is that they very rarely come to places like Belfast. They play fair enough music, but I honestly prefer the type of stuff that Christy Moore does, or the type of stuff that Clannad do, or De Danann — than that sort of Rousin' Republican balladry.'

*Gerry Adams,* Hot Press *(27 May 1983)*

'I'd been writing my own songs when I was doing the showband thing, long before Them got a record deal. "Gloria" — that was one of the first I wrote. They tell me now that "Gloria" is a classic. But it was a throwaway song. Written completely off the cuff.'

*Van Morrison,* Uncut *(July 2005)*

'It's more important to have a good session than to destroy a hotel room . . . In traditional music, there are very few rock stars, whereas in any other form of music, even classical music, it seems to be more important to look great and get all the girls rather than sit down in a room and actually play.'

*Hothouse Flowers' Peter O'Toole,* Hot Press *(15 August 1990)*

"I can't write about the upside of love without sounding cloying and insincere, so I have thrown away every genuine love song that I ever attempted to write. The sort of epigrammatic stuff I do seems to lend itself more towards taking the piss and being derogatory. I can't be flowery or poetic with a big P. Having said that, though, love has been the one side of my life that has gone really well. In fact, it's the one thing that has kept me going for the past three years or so, believe it or not. But I agree that you wouldn't think that to listen to the songs.'

*Cathal Coughlan,* Hot Press *(14 June 1990)*

'I was starving before I made *Astral Weeks* and I was still starving when it came out because I saw no money from it. I got recognition for it later, much later. But at the time, forget it. Nobody wanted to know . . . People are still debating the meaning of a song like "Madame George". Well, there's nothing to debate. "Madame George" is pure fiction. It's like a movie, a sketch, or short story. In fact, most of the songs on *Astral Weeks* are like short stories. In terms of what they mean, they're as baffling to me as anyone else. I haven't got a fucking clue what the song is about or who Madame George might have been. Those words just came through. That's what happens when you write songs. You pick up on stuff you're not even aware of. Years later, you might realise that such-and-such a line was inspired by something specific. At the time, you don't even know that, because you're picking a lot of it up sub-consciously . . . I don't remember the last time I listened to it [*Astral Weeks*]. I don't usually listen to myself . . . Why should I listen to an album like that? What it means to me is irrelevant, or should be irrelevant. It meant something to me when I was doing it. Now it doesn't matter to me in the slightest.'

*Van Morrison,* Uncut *(July 2005)*

'It was meant to be a take on Van Morrison, or maybe even a Phil Lynott take on Van Morrison, creating something slightly mythical out of the people and the suburbs where I'd grown up.'

*Bob Geldof on 'Rat Trap'*, Mojo *(May 2005)*

# CONCERTS/SHOWS

This is where it matters. You can keep your hit singles, your flop albums with just the one brilliant track, the interviews in *The Irish Times Ticket* magazine, the photo shoots in *Vanity Fair*, the chateaus in France and the Chateau Marmont in Los Angeles. You can keep your drug habits and your glasses of Pouilly Montrachet, your prescription drugs and your sunglasses. You can keep your ego in check, your smart-arsed comments in the freezer, your stupid stylised facial hair on your stupid face and your dick in your hand. You can keep your make-up, your wiggle, your insincerity, your platitudes and your psychoses. You can keep your troubles in your old kit bag, you can keep your pills in your leopard-skin pillbox and you can keep your hat on. This is where it matters: on stage, small venue, sweat, steam, eyeball-to-eyeball, rock music so loud it pins you back and rattles the fillings in your teeth. This is where it matters: on stage, open-air arena, big screen, sun cream, hot dog, cool beer, people flaking, people falling, people smiling, rock music so widescreen it blitzes the synapses. This is where it matters: on stage, intimate venue, acoustic guitar, piano, pin-dropping quiet, concentration, emotion, creativity, jokes, mistakes, singer-songwriter music so truthful and personal it makes total, perfect sense.

'U2 have had a policy over the years of giving good value . . . Our reputation for fair play was so well established that we felt the proposed ticket prices were reasonable . . . We felt that people would be interested in paying to see U2 and B. B. King performing together in a comparatively intimate setting . . . It seems we have made a mistake. We will therefore be dropping the ticket prices to IR£16 [from IR£20.50] standing and IR£18 [from IR£25.50] seating . . . As for the question of whether the shows are for charity or not, I will simply re-state U2's long-held policy of never discussing, with the media or other third parties, any charitable or philanthropic contributions we make . . . It must now be asked whether this peculiar coalition of priests and other commentators will bring their enormous influence to bear on other more essential pricing issues of the day? Petrol? The cost of travel? Should the agricultural sector be subsidised? What about interest rates? Coal and butter?'

*Paul McGuinness making a statement to* Hot Press *regarding the controversy over ticket prices for U2's Dublin shows in December 1989.*

'What I do is really acting. Singing is acting.'
*Van Morrison,* Q *(August 1993)*

# Rockaganda

'Watching someone forget the words of his own songs, that's the joy of The Pogues live . . . Offhand, I can think of about 2,000 things I'd rather see than a songwriter I admire, dying. Shane MacGowan is not a well man, something that seemed to escape all the fans who insisted on buying him drinks earlier on that day, despite the pleas of his parents. When he comes on stage, he looks the worst he possibly could, and then his appearance deteriorates.'

*Graham Linehan,* Hot Press *(21 September 1989)*

'Live, The Frames were a squealing mess, with too many hands making heavy work of material so lightweight it defied gravity, all delivered with the gravitas of someone who expected to be deified by his audience at any moment. Whatever about [Glen] Hansard, questions should have been asked in parliament about the continued presence of his female foil Noeleen, who apart from contributing the odd inaudible vocal, spent most of the time stomping around the stage with all the grace of a gorilla about to take a shit.'

*An excerpt from 'The Worst Dublin Bands In The World . . . Ever' series by George Byrne,* In Dublin *(April 10 1997)*

'Some of the tours went on too long. They didn't know how to stop doing what they'd had to do at the beginning, which was go at it non-stop. They had trouble learning to pace themselves. And, of course, managers tend to want bands to work. I think Paul sometimes overbooked them. Bands don't often have this kind of longevity, so one never knows how long you'll remain artistically and commercially viable. There's a tendency to say, "Okay, let's go for it, go for it, go for it." And because U2 are as ambitious artistically as they are, they want to keep trying things, and be out doing it. Testing the limits of how far it can go. There are a lot of good reasons for it, but sometimes it felt like it was time to stop, time to regenerate creatively, and time to give the public a rest, too. How can they miss you if you won't go away?'

*Ellen Darst, Principle Management employee from 1983–93,* U2 Show *(Orion Books 2004)*

'The Golden Horde have the most unique Dublin audience of any Irish band. With whom else would you find a bruising crew of working-class male slam–dancers uniting with a faintly psychedelic fashion–pack?'

*Excerpt from live review by Bill Graham,* Hot Press *(27 July 1989)*

'I thought the Casbah was a pit, a hellhole, a right kip, a den of iniquity. It smelled worse than a sewer and looked worse than a slaughterhouse. Its clientele were ageing hippies, poofs and prostitutes. I was appalled and shocked by its low life . . . I liked it . . .'

*Eugene Martin, one-time Undertones roadie on the famous Derry music venue,* It Makes You Want To Spit *(Reekus Music 2003)*

'There are flaws in Riverdance. The projected backdrops are rubbish . . . The narration by Planetarium Man is arrant nonsense, full of wooly Celtic drool like "No life is forever" and bollocks about the heartbeat of the soul that sounds as though it was written by Van Morrison after a midnight pickled egg feast . . . Like a dancing Pyramid of Giza, like a many-shoed Cliff Richard, *Riverdance* will last so long it may even bury Tommy. Oh, by the way, on a scale of one to infinity, it pisses all over *Cats.*'

*Review, Q (September 1996)*

'If you're getting up onstage in front of maybe a couple of thousand people who've come for a night out and you want to provoke them to think about something, you have to do it in a certain way, you have to bring them in, touch their hearts with it, rather than a confrontation . . . I love that thing that exists between a performer and the audience, that magical, intangible thing which is created. That you cannot measure or see or feel or touch. It really turns me on. Things like a good heckler. Every night something happens that has never happened before and will never happen again. It's like walking a line. Sometimes I feels quite dangerous and sometimes there's very strong emotion of different kinds. I have found myself in situations wondering if I'm going to get to the end of a song because I was being so emotionally affected. Sometimes it could be with a song that I've sung for years and years, but on a particular night something will happen. I can remember one night in the Hammersmith Odeon singing "I Pity The Poor Emigrant", and I thought I was going to choke.'

*Christy Moore,* Hot Press *(18 June 1987)*

'I watched him during rehearsal and I said, "Van, you're going to be in front of forty million people tonight." "So?" "I watched you on the monitor. During the entire rehearsal, you sang with your eyes closed." He turned to me, with his eyes closed, and said, "Why don't you just do your fuckin' job and I'll do mine?"'

*US concert promoter Bill Graham recalls a close encounter with Van Morrison,* Musician *(January 1994)*

'The annual escape from both small-town Ireland and sectarian Ulster, a weekend that's meant to be both an initiation test and a festival of fools since for once in the year, no parents or neighbours are watching.'

*Description of Féile – Trip to Tipp,* Hot Press *(27 August 1992)*

# DID THEY REALLY SAY/DO THAT?

Yes, I'm afraid they did. Just when you think that our rock stars have it sussed, that they have the measure of the world and its wily, occasionally wicked ways, they come out with a statement that is a mixture of stuff and nonsense. It's interesting to note that these people are mostly the ones that write some of the better songs we have come to hum, love and treasure over the years. Reassuringly, then, even apparently smart people come out with total bollocks. From Shane MacGowan, Sinéad O'Connor and Westlife (no surprises, there, surely?) to Enya, the Edge and Bob Geldof, it seems that we are all prone to infrequent bouts of confusion and that we should, perhaps, have stayed indoors with the locks bolted. Rock stars – you just can't talk to them but, by God, they can talk to you.

'My first serious job was as a barman in an Irish pub, a cellarman, then an apprentice barman, but I got sacked for turning up late and being pissed on the job.'
*Shane MacGowan, Q (February 1993)*

## Did They Really Say/Do That?

'I'm totally removed from reality. I remember coming out of the studio in Artane one morning after working through the night and being literally shocked to see that everything was so normal – people were going to work, going to school, laughing, talking. I had become so engrossed in what I was doing I genuinely believed there was nothing outside of that.'

*Enya,* Hot Press *(27 July 1989)*

'*Titanic* and *Patch Adams.*'

*Westlife's Kian Egan's favourite movies,* Westlife – In Real Life, *by Lisa Hand (Virgin Books 2000)*

'It'd be fair to say that absolutely nobody liked The Black Velvet Band. One damning indictment of their Darlington-like status came as part of an RTÉ Telethon in 1994, when some genius thought it'd be a good idea for the band to play in Montrose and then fly down to Cork for a free open-air gig at midnight. By the time the BVB took the stage the audience was a cider-crazed mob in no mood for tenth-rate Bob Dylan impersonators wearing designer Romany rags. In addition, they'd all been handed free candles by an insane production assistant to "add to the atmosphere". The moment [BVB singer/guitarist] Kieran Kennedy began to warble, the air was filled with flying lumps of burning wax, all captured on live television. As his hometown humiliation drew to a close, Kieran turned to a camera and screamed "Fuckin' RTÉ!", at which point the shot cut back to the studio ...'

*George Byrne,* In Dublin *(December 5 1996)*

# Rockaganda

'Apparently, my dad and I were married in a previous life. I know a lot of people are sceptical about that, but it made sense to me because we have a connection, I suppose. We don't have to speak, but we'd know what the other was thinking.'

*Chris de Burgh's daughter, Rosanna Davison,* Sunday Independent Life *magazine (February 17 2008)*

'I thought ". . . Mondays" was a b-side. I just couldn't hear the hooks. I couldn't hear the hooks on "Rat Trap" either. I don't know why that was number one.'

*Bob Geldof,* NME *(20 October 1979)*

'Every day, he calls from the Vatican looking for racing tips or greyhound results.'

*Christy Moore on being asked if he talks to Bono,* Mojo *(May 2006)*

Q: 'How come "Sunday Bloody Sunday" ended up back in the set? Didn't you vow never to play that song again?'
A (Edge): 'We lied.'

*Interview with U2,* Propaganda *(1991)*

'I couldn't believe it caused such a fuss – I certainly didn't mean it to. See, because I grew up with so many brothers, I've always worn trousers and I absolutely hate dresses. Wedding dresses are the worst! Why would I want to get married looking like a lampshade or a meringue? So I decided to wear this slight over-dress thing and some knickers to cover my bum and pubes area. And, anyway, I've tiny boobs - I'm, like, a 34A, or whatever - so I was hardly spilling out everywhere.'

*Dolores O'Riordan on her wedding attire,* Q *(April 1999)*

'It's not a biography. It's just a garbled bunch of tapes of me out of my brains talking to my missus, yeah?'

*Shane MacGowan's opinion of his 2001 semi-autobiography,* A Drink With Shane MacGowan, *as quoted in* The Word *(January 2005)*

'I was abused from the moment I was conceived.'

'It is historically proven that the Roman Catholic Church assassinated Jesus Christ.'

'Adolf Hitler wasn't a bad person, he was just a fucked-up person.'

'I thought the Los Angeles riots were great . . .'

'That woman who is suing Mike Tyson is a bitch. I don't care if he raped her.'

'If Princess Diana ran the world − which she has the power to do − child abuse wouldn't exist anymore.'

'Sorry for going on. We all get a bit bonkers in this business.'

*A selection of quotes from Sinéad O'Connor,* Q *(January 1993)*

'I've developed a virus that only destroys U2 albums and is so persistent − it's like a musical ebola − that it can destroy every written down lyric, every analogue and digital copy of a U2 song. It can even eat into the brains of Bono and The Edge and destroy the next song they're going to write. I've got it here in a little bottle.'

*Writer Will Self,* NME *(23 February 2008)*

'Adam was sitting up in a tree throwing down apples at his parents like a spoilt child. The Edge was cleaning out a pigeon loft. Bono was running down the road with jumpers wrapped around his belly. He was being chased 'cos he'd done an orchard. McGuinness was looking out a window at him with a scowl on his face. All this time Larry is sitting alone in a room with church-like windows made out of ice.'

*Stano's dream about U2,* Hot Press *(4 May 1989)*

'I can't say it bothers me because . . . it happens . . . but I'd love to sit down with everybody that comes to the show and go, OK, I know everybody's got a different idea of what to expect but, you know when you feel that urge to go, Wurrghh? Well actually, sometimes it doesn't suit. Especially when it's really delicate and 80 per cent of the audience want that moment because they're hanging on it. It's like somebody farting on the Tube: you can't stop them doing it, it's just nicer if they don't.'

*Damien Rice on his fans singing along to his songs,* Q *(April, 2004)*

'For a while Bono was Bon Smelly Arse. I was glad that didn't stick, or things might have been different. I don't know if the band could have got very far with a singer called Bon Smelly Arse.'

*Edge on early band member nicknames,* U2 By U2 *(October 2006)*


'I can remember staying in Feargal Sharkey's mum's house. I was put in the guest bedroom. I walked in there and here were all these pictures of the Last Supper and a Sacred Heart picture. I remember thinking, "fuck, I wish I'd been a Catholic". But the next morning, when Feargal came up to the room with an Ulster fry, I said to Feargal this is the first time in my life I'm proud to be a Prod, how the fuck could you have a wank in this room?"'

*Terri Hooley,* It Makes You Want To Spit *(Reekus Music 2003)*


'It was the Craggy Island factor that people never quite got about The Boomtown Rats. You had the [Sex] Pistols singing about no future, because they were just waking up to an England where you might not be able to get a decent job. So what? I came from a country where a genius like Flann O'Brien could spend a whole life in the civil service. What were these punks complaining about? As far as I was concerned, I was in this to get laid and make money . . . In Ireland, antagonism had worked wonders for the Rats' profile, so I felt no need to change. Also, I was that bit older. So at a time when you had to be ideological, everything had to be polarized. The Clash were the good guys and everything that had gone before sucked. Excuse me? The Clash? A load of middle-class geezers dressed by

## Rockaganda

Jasper Conran and living by Regents Park! Their first gig? In a small room for invited journalists! Very revolutionary. That stuff drove me round the fucking twist.'

*Bob Geldof,* Mojo *(May 2005)*

# FAME/SUCCESS/WEALTH

It isn't what they enter the world of rock music for – or at least that's what most of them say (Bob Geldof being the notable exception: he has famously stated that he wanted to get into rock music to get rich and get laid. Result!). And so pretty much all of them start off in a haze of innocence and poverty. Then, slowly, after a few years, the money starts rolling in, the on-tour accommodation gets upgraded from bus to B&B to 3-star twin-bed to four-star single room to 5-star suite. The vice of choice might change, too: from guzzling a few innocent beers in the back of the van to the nastiness of shoving crudely-cut cocaine up your nose. True friends come and go, replaced on an ad hoc basis by leeches that only want to be associated with you so that they can bask in the reflected glory of your success and wealth. Some rock stars become wrapped up in their own myths, believe their approved press releases and generally turn into the kind of person they hated with a vengeance twenty years before (moral: be careful what you wish for, as it could turn around years later and bite you on the arse). Some simply don't know what to do with it – the very thought of engaging with the public outside a concert performance is anathema to them. Others use their success and wealth wisely. Others want to, and blow it big-time. Others crave it and will do virtually anything to get it. And the people who say fame/success/ wealth isn't all it's cracked up to be have no idea what they're talking about. Give it to me, then – I'd know what to do with it.

'His house was crawling with creeps. They all thought they were his best friend but they were just leeches.'

*Frank Murray, former Thin Lizzy road manager on 'friends' of Phil Lynott,* Mojo *(December 1993)*

'This was a different crowd to what we had seen before, not a cliquey fashion crowd, but punks from the Antrim Road, the Ormeau, the Shankill, the Falls. Mummy didn't collect these kids afterwards – they fought their way out at night and fought their way home again. This was our crowd and we quickly developed a large following.'

*The Outcasts bassist, Greg Cowan,* It Makes You Want To Spit *(Reekus Music 2003)*

'Some composers can get a million dollars for a film, but I'm still a baby in this world. I was paid handsomely for *Out Of Sight, Oceans* and *Analyze That*, though you don't retain your publishing for those major movies so it's not as much as you might think. And it's highly pressurized when you're working on such big budget films. I could go down that road of doing any big movie that I'm offered, sell my soul and become very wealthy very quickly. But I just can't do it. I turned down 60 scripts after *Out Of Sight*, because they just felt wrong. I want to work on films that I believe in, so my next two soundtracks are very low budget affairs and won't seriously alter my bank balance, although I will get the publishing, which means that at least I'll earn whenever there's a repeat on telly or whatever.'

*David Holmes, Belfast DJ-turned-Hollywood-soundtrack composer,* The Word *(May 2003)*

'I just can't handle it, and I've never been able to handle it, and I never will. There were times when I thought I needed to do this, that and the other thing, where I could handle it, but it didn't go anywhere. I don't really want to be celebrated. You know? I just want to do the music. And celebrity is another loaded word. It isn't what it appears to be.'

*Van Morrison,* Q *(April 1997)*

The relationship between Geldof and Columbia cooled quickly as his mouthy impulse returned to effectively put the blinkers on their America adventure. Geldof was assured there would be fans at their March '79 San Diego co-headliner with The Fabulous Poodles – but for the main part it was a showcase to which all the US programme directors had been flown in: 'You could break America tonight, says our radio plugger. I sort of know what's at stake so I'm nervous. As we leave the hotel to go to the gig,

I'm told by Fachtna, our manager, to share a car with this guy in a satin Foreigner jacket. Now, I don't know why, but when I'm told that someone's important to my career it's like a red rag to a bull. So I get in the fucking car with this guy and the first thing he says is, "Hey! Are you with The Boomtown Poodles?" I'm fucking incensed. My vanity is mortally offended; and this klutz is on a freebie and I've got to share a taxi with him. Halfway through the show, it's time to do "Rat Trap" – at which point I get a flash of satin jacket at the back. And that's enough. I say, Just a minute. Can you turn on the lights? What do you think of radio in America? And all these kids in the audience were like, "It fucking sucks, man!" So I said, Well, you're going to tell the people who programme what you hear exactly what you think of them. See those guys up there, by the balcony? They're all DJs and radio people. So the crowd turn around and start shouting, "You fucking assholes!" That night we're off the air on 60 major stations across America. After the show, Fingers [Johnny, Boomtown Rats keyboard player] recalls walking off to see their newly appointed radio plugger, who had previously broken Aerosmith in America, in tears. I remember him saying, "Do you realise what Bob has done? It's the end of you in America".'

*Bob Geldof,* Mojo *(May 2005)*

Ray Harmon: 'I'm willing to invest it all on having Limerick turned upside down and a shrubbery planted on top.'

Alan Byrne: 'I'd buy shares in Brylcream.'

Eamonn Ryan: 'I owe it already.'

Tom Dunne: 'I'd spend it on destroying as many non-vital organs as are capable of giving me pleasure and seeking medical advice on the others.'

*Something Happens on being asked how they would spend their first million,* Hot Press *(20 April 1989)*

'I'd like to see us in the Top 20 in Britain. I'd love to see us in the US charts. I'd like to see the band more widely accepted, even if we haven't got these hits. I'd like to see the band a helluva lot bigger. I'd like to see Ireland appreciating Les Enfants for what they are, for how good they are now and how good they can be if they're given the chance. I'd like to see Derek Herbert become less arrogant and less conceited in the public eye, but still as strong, still as powerful. I don't know whether people are afraid of me, or whether they hate me . . . I'd like to see people accepting me more as a person . . . If they ever took the time to look at me on stage, to look at me singing songs, then they'd know I'm not the arrogant, conceited bastard they think I am. I want to climb to the top. I want to see what it's like up there. I want to see what it's like looking down. I'm sick of looking up.'

*Les Enfants lead singer, Derek Herbert,* Hot Press *(5 October 1984)*

'Fame and beauty together have proved to be a curse for me. Fame especially. It's the reason I keep leaving the game. I find it painful, I really do. To be a good artist you need to be terribly sensitive. If you are sensitive then you're not well suited to the vileness of the music industry. If you don't do what you're told all the time, everyone treats you as a difficult fucking artist . . . You know what the best thing about being famous is? It's the money. Or rather the freedom that money provides.'

*Sinéad O'Connor,* Uncut *(July 2007)*

'Anyone who's famous sometimes wishes they were anonymous, and I'm no exception.'

*Van Morrison,* Mojo *(April 2006)*

'If I never sell another record in America I wouldn't lose any sleep over it. I can honestly say I prefer playing in Kerry rather than America. If I get an American release and sell 100,000 records there'd be nobody more pleased than me. But it's not an ambition because I learned from way back — I've been kicked in the teeth so often with Moving Hearts and Planxty. If you lean back so far to achieve certain things, you lose what you had in the first place.'

*Christy Moore,* Hot Press *(18 June 1987)*

'I wouldn't be an artist for nothing. Success is nothing if you don't have something to show for it. Mozart didn't have a penny when he died . . . So talent doesn't mean you'll be successful. There are an awful lot of really successful people out there who are mediocre at what they do.'

*Caroline Corr,* Q *(July 1999)*

'Referring to U2's Bono and The Edge, who have joined forces with Paddy McKillen for the latest scheme, he [conservationist Michael Smith] writes: "The common good is not served by allowing the richest people in Ireland to build with the benefit of tax incentives only to demolish when they get bored." Smith claims that their interest in redeveloping The Clarence [Hotel] "now owes more to a fetish for glamour", saying that they "still haven't found what they are looking for . . . Unfortunately for its owners, the Clarence Hotel is not a pair of sunglasses or a hat."'
*Property Section,* The Irish Times *(10 January 2008)*

'A million albums (sold) doesn't mean a million pounds. But I don't worry about my rent. I spend all my money on music, films and books. I have no hobbies. I don't drive. I don't like gadgets outside my iPod and laptop.'
*Gary Lightbody (Snow Patrol),* Q *(April 2007)*

'I was getting offered deals, and basically saying "No, I've got a little contract with myself." There are so many doors opening to us, and the surreal part is like: I couldn't really give a fuck. I don't want to be famous, I don't crave any of these things. I don't crave fame – or any of the things that fame brings. I get enough from playing on stage to ten people or three people or 500 people. I don't like getting into the places that you can "get into" by being famous.'
*Damien Rice,* Hot Press *(24 September 2003)*

'I don't regard myself as a Top Twenty musician at all. I just want to continue playing. I just want to be able to walk into a shop and buy a bar of chocolate, or go into a bar and have a pint without being besieged all the time . . . I don't want to get into the Rolls-Royce and the mansion and the cloak-and-dagger sort of living.'

*From* Irish Tour, *Tony Palmer's 1974 documentary of Rory Gallagher's 1973 tour of Ireland.*

'I really hate people who carp at fame. Look at me. A beautiful house, a beautiful car, a beautiful family. I would recommend this way of life. Who'd have possibly thought it? . . . I didn't have the image for a (rock) band. I didn't have long hair, I looked like a teenyboy popper and wore what I thought were trendy clothes. Pop was perfect for how I looked and for my attitude. I wasn't a serious artist, come on, I was a young guy that liked singing. I couldn't play an instrument. I thought I could write some poems which could try to be songs, but by no means was I a cool artist.'

*Ronan Keating,* Q *(September 2000)*

'Work hard, make good records; get the records heard and the people in the bands seen. They've got to get out there and hustle — sell yourself that way . . . For starters, they've got to want to be successful, and that means being ready for all that success can give them — the constant travelling, make-up, media presence, promotion, the highs and lows. They have to sacrifice their own personal life for it, too. They're public property, and they've got to realise that. It's part of the game, the price to pay for being rich and famous.'

*Louis Walsh,* Cara Magazine *(July 2002)*

'She's changed . . . I don't know what's happened to her head. She always had some funny ideas. When she sang some backing vocals for Moose [now defunct indie band], she didn't do it for free. She then spent the next couple of weeks ringing me up asking when she was going to get paid for it. She was very interested in money.'
*The Cranberries' former publicist John Best on Dolores O'Riordan, Q (October 1994)*

'The access–all–areas aspect of the dream – I still want that. In those countries where we haven't done it I still feel this . . . need . . . to do it as I did here at the beginning. I feel driven to maintain what we've got, and I still feel a keen sense of competition. Everything to me is potential competition and must be viewed in that light. I don't know if I have any more ambitions , but I have a lot of dreams. Ambitions are things you'll probably attain: a dream is something that you hope you'll attain . . . If your ambition is to get to number one, when you get there you've achieved that ambition. I don't think the dream that I had at the beginning has been attained, but a lot of the ambitions have been.'
*Bob Geldof, NME (20 October 1979)*

'After ten years saving the whale, it's like, forget the whale, remember the bank account!'
*Larry Mullen Jr, Vogue (December 1992)*

'I cherish the fact that we're still mates, but I always have the memory of him as this fucker from up the road. He's

like a brother but we're chalk and cheese. I've seen a lot, so I'm not an eejit, but I couldn't handle 15 million sales.'
*Gavin Friday,* Q *(April 1992)*

'Success? It's not all that important. I love music and I'm lucky enough to be selling albums. I could be sitting in my bedroom writing songs that nobody could care less about, or buy, but I don't want that. I want people to buy my records on a worldwide scale. Not because it brings flash cars and big houses, but to prove to people that I can do it.'
*Ronan Keating,* Cara Magazine *(March 2001)*

'I'd worked with Peter Gabriel on the *Birdy* soundtrack and the *So* album – I think the day we began *The Joshua Tree*, "Sledgehammer" was Number 1 in America. I remember walking in with a tray of tea, Edge looked at me and said, "It's Dan! We're going to be rich!"'
The Joshua Tree *producer Daniel Lanois,* Mojo *(January 2008)*

'They're clapping you and your songs: they know the words. I defy anyone not to be flattered by that.'
*Bob Geldof,* NME *(20 October 1979)*

'I'm always pulling on the handbrakes. When something goes too fast, you can miss what's passing by out the window. It's like going on a plane: if you've got a functional reason for going somewhere it's great, but you experience a lot more by driving. And then, if you get out of the car and walk that 100 metres that you zipped by, you could stop, sit on the ground and pull the grass apart and there's a universe going on in there, you know. So society says it's great to be big. But being big can take away from the specialness . . . The growth thing, it's like a cafe. You open up a really cool little organic vegetarian cafe, and there's a certain type of people that come to it and you really bond with them. And then it gets popular and you wonder if you should make it bigger or open up another one. It's a question of knowing when to stop, knowing when you lose what you had originally. And I'm just watching it at the moment because it's precious.'

*Damien Rice, Q (April 2004)*

'We're not quite Hanson and we're not quite Michael Jackson. But we were at the right age when we first got our success, so we coped with it okay. We were also at the age that when things went wrong and we had the drinking problems after the first album, we could bounce back and it made us stronger.'

*Tim Wheeler, Ash, Q (October 2002)*

'I remember one time, at the end of the tour, we're travelling home and I'm sitting beside him on the plane and he says to me, "So what are you doing when you get back home?" "I'm off to America with this band, Patrick Street." And he says, "You're so fucking lucky, man. You can do that. I can't do that. If I went into that band, I'd fuck [it] up. On the second gig there'd be a queue of people at the door. I'd fuck up the band because I'm Van Morrison. I can't do what you do." And it was absolutely true, what he said . . . Van fought for a while with trying to do small things – being the common man and play[ing] himself down – but it's too late for him. [It was about] a year after he said that to me that he realised, "Fuck it! I have to be 'Van'. I can't be anybody else." [So now] he wears his hat and his black glasses. I think it's sort of sad.'

*Musician Arty McGlynn,* Can You Feel The Silence? A New Biography of Van Morrison *by Clinton Heylin (Viking Books 2002)*

'I was surprised by the success of my albums, I still am. I wasn't making records to win awards or to get famous. When you're young those things can be stressful. I found it took me away from my own life, from things I wanted to do for my own spiritual development. I found it hard being a pop star. It meant that I couldn't do my own private life, instead I had to go to do MTV awards and stuff which didn't really mean shit to me. It also meant putting my recovery on hold. I'd had quite a difficult upbringing so I think becoming famous so young put a stop to me recovering from that.'

*Sinéad O'Connor,* Cara Magazine *(October 2002)*

'Hey, man! I'm rich and I'm only 22. I've got so much money, I have to put it all straight into my bank account, I can't handle it!'

*Dolores O'Riordan,* Q *(March 1994)*

## Fame/Success/Wealth

'I never understood it then and I don't understand it now.'
*Feargal Sharkey on being asked did it bother him that The Undertones never achieved significant commercial success,* In Dublin *(23 May 1991)*

'I want to be famous and successful – I've been that way since I was about eight. Since I saw Michael Jackson.'
*Ash's Tim Wheeler,* Q *(October 1995)*

'Alan [Downey] became the accountant [of the band] because he's the only one of us who got his Leaving Certificate.'
*Aslan's Christy Dignam,* D'Side *(August/September 1994)*

'Wake up at about 4 a.m. with a terrifying sadness that later subsides to a vague depression. I tried to analyse it but I can never remember dreams . . . After the gig we stayed at the club. I got tired about 2 a.m. and was lying on the pool table staring up at the small blue disco lights that chased each other across the black ceiling. Over my head, the fluorescent tube hummed and I felt like I was in a Scorsese film. Hippy girls flitted like tie-dyed moths around the edge of the halo of light and passed joints and bottles of exotic oils for me to smell. One handed me a cheesecloth D'Artagnan floppy-type shirt as a gift. Occasionally, a bouncer's face would loom directly overhead close, pores lit huge by the neon, smelling pretty and asking for an autograph. Or a Chippendale-type blue bow-tied barman asking me to take the local beer, rum, Shiraz, whatever. I took them all and in the oppressive night heat, I realised I was 41, on the Tropic of Capricorn and lived a life few people are able to. I turned out lucky. At the end of the table, an 18-year old hippy said she was into reflexology and could she rub my feet? Bathed in sweat I lay back exhausted while this jingle-jangle angel rubbed and kneaded my veiny, nobbled, sneaker-stinking plates like a henna-haired Magdalen. God bless her . . . There's some fan in the lobby. She came up from the gig last night. She sent a tape to the room. It's shit. She's bright-eyed with hope and joy and nerve. I say, "It's great." "Really?" "Yeh, really, it's fantastic." "You're so fantastic," she says. "You're my inspiration." My depression is now complete.'

*An excerpt from Bob Geldof's Australian tour diary,* Q *(June 1994)*

'Timing is a huge thing, and anybody who's been successful in music would be foolish to say that luck didn't come into it at several points. We all know of great bands that made great records, but for whatever reasons it just didn't happen. We were lucky, no doubt about that.'

*Thrills guitarist Daniel Ryan,* Cara Magazine *(September 2004)*

'People are obsessed with my money! It's really no big deal, you know. It's something you get used to. And, alright, I know I'm fairly rich, but I think that £30m is a bit of an exaggeration. I remember when we made our first million. Me and the boys went mad crazy with it, buying loads of clothes and presents. It was a grand feeling . . . But you get used to it very quickly. I think it would be different if we'd won the lottery, but we didn't. Sure, we're well paid for what we do, but we've earned this money, every penny of it.'

*Dolores O'Riordan,* Q *(April 1999)*

'I really don't care whether I'm a star or not. I never wanted to be a star in the first pace, but I think a lot of these so-called stars like the lifestyle and can't really do it without being a star. So they don't want to expose something that supports them.'

*Van Morrison,* Mojo *(August 1995)*

'People ask for autographs here and it drives me mad. They do it for collections, just in case you get big. They actually have no idea who you are. Celebrity is their monarch.'

*Andrea Corr,* Q *(July 1999)*

'My aim, my plan, is longevity, which the polar opposite to the present pop climate. I want to be around for ages. I know I can. I love to be good at what I do. People don't want to be good at what they do anymore. They just want to be famous.'

*Ronan Keating,* The Irish Times *Magazine (27 April 2002)*

# WIT

It's all very well being funny on stage with those well rehearsed quips; it's all very well being amusing around the dinner table, lobbing one-liners here and zingers there as the hosts open up one bottle of wine after another. But the truth is unless you do comedy for a living (and if it doesn't come naturally, how laborious that would be), there's a fine line between making people laugh and making people yawn – the mouth is open but for very different reasons. Besides, wit, or humour – or whatever you wish to call it – is quite a peculiarly personal thing. We all want to be seen as amusing, though, which is why even the grumpiest of rock star occasionally attempts to crack a joke in order to get the party started. Isn't that right, Van? What a marvellous night for a moondance? Don't think so.

'I hate those guys in interviews that say, "Come and see the band and buy all the records". They always sound so insincere. So I'd like to say, really sincerely, come and see the band and buy all the records.'

*Phil Lynott,* Hot Press *(18 May 1984)*

'The only man in Europe who doesn't fancy The Corrs.'

*Comedy writer Arthur Matthews on Jim Corr, as quoted in* Q *(July 1999)*

'Aidan, has your sex life improved since you became a megastar?'

'Oh no, it's got much better!'

*Aidan Walsh,* Hot Press *(December 1987)*

'It's the line that puts the fear of God in all of us.'

*Bono on Paul McGuinness's infamous eight-word request: "I have someone I'd like you to meet",* U2: At the End of the World, *by Bill Flanagan (Bantam Press 1995)*

U2 Joke:

Q: How many members of U2 does it take to change a lightbulb?

A: Just one. Bono holds the light bulb and the world revolves around him.

Q *(June 1995)*

'Er . . . you mean attacked? A couple of times people have said something, but we buried them shortly after.'

*Phil Lynott on being asked was he verbally or physically abused because of his colour,* Hot Press *(18 May 1984)*

'If Bono left we could carry on. If I left we'd be screwed.'
*Larry Mullen Jr,* Mojo *(July 2005)*

'Show us your tits.'
'Show me your balls if you got any.'
*Repartee between an audience member and Ireland's one-time hard rocking female April South,* Hot Press *(13 May 1983)*

'If he'd been around today Phil [Lynott] would have been straight into The Priory [UK rehab clinic], even if it was just to pull Kate Moss! And he'd have probably chinned Pete Doherty, too, and done us all a favour!'
*Former Thin Lizzy guitarist Gary Moore,* Mojo *(February 2006)*

'Favourite Saying: "Send him a large fish, wrapped in a newspaper."
Greatest ambition: "To intern all bad poets."'
*U2 manager Paul McGuinness,* Hot Press *(9 February 1989)*

# WISDOM

It's different from being overtly smart or intellectual; wisdom is the cumulative effect of life's experiences and how we respond to any given situation via stored and shared memories. Curiously enough, there appears to be a lot of wisdom around these parts, from Bono's statement about going out to dinner too often with people on the payroll and former Fat Lady Sings frontman Nick Kelly going on about the virus that is ART to Bob Geldof's quite foreboding worldview and Ronan Keating's acceptance of his diminishing public profile (the admission of which, when you think about it, is very wise indeed). Unlike wit, however, wisdom is rarely viewed in a subjective manner; wisdom is as wisdom does and is viewed as such by the vast majority of people. We don't need anyone to tell us that it is wise to be inherently content with your lot in life, or that if/when the splash of success dries up it is perhaps best to bid a fond goodbye to it rather than desperately try to maintain it at whatever cost to dignity and integrity. Or to admit that there are such things in life as responsibilities. Not very rock 'n' roll, but there you go . . .

❖

'"Ah yes, but we were being ironic" – that was our fuckin' *raison d'être*. It was our answer to everything. We didn't rationalize things at all and we didn't understand how we were being perceived, and we suffered for that. Of course, back then we also secured ourselves in a cocoon by thinking that everything was crap – music, books, you name it. We ended up being disconnected from everything that was happening around us. Now I see the stupidity of that . . . Another big problem was that there was a large section of our audience that I wasn't particularly enamoured with. A lot of them seemed to have that disease that afflicts people in their twenties, the need to be "ironic" and bury your grievances under a slick veneer. There was all this crap about ritual encores and I was expected to be some sort of Morrissey dickhead, which I never was. I know a lot of it was our own fault but Jesus, it pissed me off.'

*Cathal Coughlan,* Hot Press *(14 June 1990)*

'I'm no more a tragic or disturbed figure than anybody else. I think there's a great arrogance amongst other artists that they would see their suffering as being far more intense than anybody else's. The only thing that's more intense is the genuinely perverse desire to share it with other people. To me it's the virus that is "Art". This virus

is really what makes you want to take your diary and throw it to other people as some form of screw-up.'
*Nick Kelly [then of The Fat Lady Sings], In Dublin (23 May 1991)*

'If you're going out for dinner four times a week and you look round the table and everybody's on your payroll, then you've probably become a prick.'
*Bono, Q (February 2002)*

'I had to leave [the band]. It was exhaustion and a lot of other things that were available. On one side I had my health problem and on the other side I had a chance to make a lot of money and a lot of fame and everything that goes with it, which I'd worked for all my life. I chose my health, which was more important.'
*Thin Lizzy's Eric Bell, Mojo (December 1993)*

'I get frightened by all these bands who are so positive about everyone, they're worried that if they say anything they'll upset a Nirvana fan and then *their* album won't sell. Just say no, and then think about [saying] yes very slowly.'
*Gavin Friday, Q (April 1992)*

'I'm a very slow songwriter. In 1995, we did about three gigs, and I wrote about two new songs. This year we've been a bit busier – we recorded an album that didn't get released, and have played about fifteen gigs so far. As is quite obvious, we're not out there battling for a major

record deal. We're all sufficiently involved and interested in other areas of activity that we're happy enough to leave it that way. I'd love to do it full-time, bring out records, tour, but at 33 I find I have to be realistic about these things. I'm no spring chicken and I have responsibilities.'
*The Revenants' Stephen Ryan,* The Irish Times *(20 November 1996)*

'It's 5 a.m. We are driving through Nenagh and everyone in the van is in a post-gig, alcohol-induced sleep apart from myself and, thankfully, the van driver. A lot of things go through one's mind at times like this. Three years ago, I was being picked up from Munich Airport and driven to the Hilton Hotel where champagne awaited my arrival, courtesy of the record company. One year later I was signing on the dole in Camden Town. Am I supposed to take any of this seriously? So what is the continued attraction of this thing called rock 'n' roll? Is it the chance to rebel and fly in the face of convention? Don't make me laugh. This is an age when politicians everywhere have a monopoly on sex scandals, bishops get charged with drunken driving, athletes get convicted of drug trafficking and stockbrokers are football hooligans. On the other hand, rock stars are saving the ozone layer/rainforests/political prisoners, eating macrobiotic food, working out, getting sponsored by multi-nationals, and being presented in some cases as role models for an entire nation/generation. Is the attraction the chance to change things? Well, if you want to change the world you should get into either television or politics. Rock and roll doesn't change the world, the world changes anyway . . . If the attraction is drugs you should become an advertising executive or an athlete. If you are caught you can blame the doctor who prescribed them. If the attraction is fame you should become an actor and join a soap opera. You will also find it easier to have a hit record that way.'

*Musician Ronan O'Hanlon, formerly guitarist with Les Enfants and The Word,* Hot Press *(22 February 1990)*

'I always wonder how I'm going to die. Will I go quietly in my sleep, will I get mangled by a car and lie there screaming or maybe it'll be some cancerous thing. It's going to happen and it's final. I'm not concerned with immortality, because if I believed in the Catholic concept of eternity I'd be so frightened that I couldn't handle it. Immortality doesn't bother me. If people have forgotten about "I Don't Like Mondays" two weeks from now, *no problem.* I've never considered immortality in terms of rock and roll. I don't think rock songs should be remembered. It's a twentieth-century art form, it's here and then it's superceded. Immortality doesn't interest me. I'm purely concerned with the here and now. I reckon that if you're aware that you've only got a few years to do it, you end up with a fairly pessimistic viewpoint about most things. I've got fairly gloomy ideas.'

*Bob Geldof,* NME *(20 October 1979)*

'Your nature is a very hard thing to change; it takes time. One of the extraordinary transferences that happen in your spiritual life is not that your character flaws go away

but they start to work for you. A negative becomes a positive: you've a big mouth: you end up a singer. You're insecure: you end up a performer who needs applause. I have heard of people having life-changing, miraculous turnarounds, people set free from addiction after a single prayer, relationships saved where both parties "let go, and let God". But it was not like that for me. For all that "I was lost, I am found" [a line from the U2 song, "Gloria"], it is probably more accurate to say, "I was really lost, I'm a little less so at the moment." And then a little less and a little less again . . . The slow reworking and rebooting of a computer at regular intervals, reading the small print of the service manual. It has slowly rebuilt me in a better image. It has taken years, though, and it is not over yet.'
*Bono,* U2 By U2 *(2006)*


'I accepted it [decrease in profile] more or less overnight – from the hysteria of being in a boy band and arriving at airports with thousands of people waiting for you to the next day being a solo artist and that level of hysteria disappearing. It was unbelievable, that overnight thing, which is strange because I'm selling more records in a solo capacity. Things like that make you change and make you tougher. I pinch myself most of the times . . . I love it, I have to say. Far from it I was raised, indeed, and I'm very lucky to still be here. I've seen so many people come and go in the past nine years and have still managed to maintain a certain level of success and comfort. I'm not extravagant in that I demand a certain level of hotel room, or this studio or that car. If anything pulled up outside the door of my house to drive me to somewhere I'd get in and go to work. I know I'm lucky to be where I am.'

*Ronan Keating,* The Irish Times Magazine *(27 April 2002)*


'I'm perfectly happy with who I am . . . That's possibly what pisses people off. I hear them say, "The guy is so happy with what he is – God, what a bastard."'

*Chris de Burgh,* Hot Press *(1 December 1988)*

# WELL, I NEVER!

Occasionally, wisdom goes out the window on a very long walk to a place where borderline insanity lives. Has anyone ever said something that they had thought was quite witty, but which in the cold light of day they uncovered not a scintilla of humour? Has anyone ever said anything that to all intents and purposes contained many seeds of wisdom only to find out fairly quickly that the seeds contained a virus? It's a potent reminder to us mere mortals that on more than one occasion our favourite Irish rock stars have come out with the most incredible tripe. In a gob-smacking blend of pseudo-intellectual ramblings, bald statements on a variety of subjects, head-scratching non-sequiturs, verbal surreality and common-or-garden grade-A manure, it is clear that the Irish rock star is multi-layered beast. We like them (in fact, we love some of them), but by God they can occasionally come out with more garbage than a landfill. As you read on, you will ask yourself the questions: is this really the same person who wrote one of my favourite, most expressive, most eloquent, most poignant, most personal songs? Is this really the same person whose lyrics have made me shed silent tears every time I hear my favourite, most expressive, most eloquent, most poignant, most personal song? The answer is yes. And yes.

'Sean O'Hagan can vividly remember being kicked off the U2 Boy tour. He was the guitarist in Microdisney, an angry band from Cork whose grammar frequently verged on the inflammatory. Never more so than at the tour's Dublin gig, when singer Cathal Coughlan's soundcheck went, in full: "The U2 boy wanks and sniffs glue."'
Q *(August 1995)*

'There was the lunch at the Westbury Hotel conducting an interview . . . Or rather there was me sitting across a table watching (Van) Morrison dribbling slithery coleslaw down his chin onto his bib and insulting me . . . "That's a stupid fucking question . . . I'm not fucking answering that." . . . His final spasm of boorishness came in the form of an observation that: "I'm not fucking here to answer questions." Eventually, I upped and swept out in what I desperately hoped was a flurry of dignity. Outside, I had the pleasure of telling him to fuck off when, propelled by his record label's publicist, he came running to plead with me to come back . . . And then there was the night in Bad Bob's . . . when, in a moment of madness, mistaking a grimace for a grin, I asked him whether, as a gesture towards political correctness, he might like henceforth to be known as Van the Person. The scowl remained affixed to his face by rawl plugs for the rest of the night. Van's

manager at the time, Paul Charles, accosted me at the tail-
end of the evening with an accusation that I had "ruined
Van's whole night". It was only a joke, I pleaded. "Are ye
mad? A joke? Van doesn't do jokes".'
*Eamon McCann,* Hot Press *(15 June 2005)*

'God, I've been wondering who this Luciano is all day. I
didn't know he was the same bloke as Pavarotti.'
*Boyzone's Keith Duffy,* Q *(August 1999)*

'The chieftain of our country'
*Oscar winner Glen Hansard on Bono. Hansard had just received
a text message from the U2 frontman congratulating him on the
Oscar win. Receiving a text from Bono, said Hansard, 'is one of
the biggest things that can happen to an Irishman.'* The Irish
Times *(26 February 2008)*

'"There's 57 different varieties." That's a song.'
*Van Morrison,* Mojo *(August 1995)*

'Kate Bush is a woman, I'm a woman, we both have
breasts . . .'
*Sinéad O'Connor,* Hot Press *(November 1987)*

'You know that you're never allowed to shit on the tour
bus because it's the poor driver who has to clean it out
after you've left? He'll always tell you to request a shit stop
whenever you have to go. But us lot are always too shy to

ask him to pull over, so one of us – in fact, all of us at some point – ends up sneaking a sly one. But you're asking for trouble, because as the shit mounts up, then, Jaysus, the stink of it is enough to knock you out!'

*Dolores O'Riordan, Q (April 1999)*

'There used to be a street-singer-cum-comedian style chappie round about Wexford at the turn of the century and his name was Johnny Patterson and he was famous for lots of songs including "The Stone Outside Dan Murphy's Door" and "The Garden Where The Praties Grow". The first time I heard The Pogues I was put in mind of Johnny – except not so much the real Johnny but Bizarro Johnny, the kind you might meet if Johnny had ever made an appearance in DC *Superman* comics along with Mr Mxylpltk. Where his face would look like it was made of broke-up bricks and instead of making children's parties memorable and fun to attend, he would be wrecking them, setting fire to curtains, etc – for no apparent reason whatsoever. Then he would laugh – but not an ordinary laugh but one that was like one you'd expect to hear out of Balor Of The Evil Eye or someone with a rocket shoved up his hole.'

*Writer Patrick McCabe, an excerpt from his sleeve notes to the reissued album,* Peace & Love *(Warner Strategic Marketing 2004)*

'Many of the letters we get are from girls of the middle-class variety who live in Surrey. But we also get letters from this guy called Uncle Percy Sunglasses who lives in

Birmingham. He tells Sean [O'Hagan, Coughlan's Microdisney colleague] at the end of his letters that he loves him. But he doesn't seem to like anything we do! He tells us we're brilliant and then he criticizes every single song.'

*Cathal Coughlan reveals the confused public perceptions of Microdisney.* Hot Press *(15 February 1985)*

'I tell you what, if Ken Livingstone was still around, your balls wouldn't be freezing off ya in the Albert Hall. Shirley Bassey told me that.'

*Christy Moore,* Mojo *(January/February 1994)*

'Play tight head prop for Ireland, ride a winner at the Curragh, break 60 in snooker, do the Liffey swim, walk the Cliffs of Moher with Baroness Thatcher and be able to sing "When A Man Loves A Woman".'

*Christy Moore on being asked what were his unfulfilled ambitions,* Mojo *(May 2006)*

'There was the crazed acidhead who'd sit in your front garden drawing diagrams of what they were going to do to you sexually when they got you. Guys who thought we were married in a past life and stuff.'

*Sinéad O'Connor on obsessive fans,* Mojo *(October 2005)*

'To continually be yourself when you're in the spotlight is very difficult, and it's very easy to fall into the traps that are there. It's like going to a concert and thinking that it was brilliant, then going the next night and hearing the guy do exactly the same ad-libs and giving the same shit to the crowd. You go "Fuck, that guy's been wanking me off" . . .'

*The 4 of Us frontman, Brendan Murphy,* Hot Press *(8 February 1990)*

'A *Village Voice* journalist reviewed a Princess Tinymeat compilation album and came up with the conclusion that I was the true queen of pop, comparing me with Madonna. Now, the comparison I could go for, because it got me out of the indie ethic. But then the writer ended up with the hoary old comparison to Boy George. He wrote, "Boy George is a gender-bender, Binttii is a screaming faggot. The last Princess Tinymeat single was called "Put It There", and there's a lyric in it that goes, "I have a tape measure, it'll tell you how much I'm going to like you". Now, I really didn't see this as a phallic expression, but this writer said about it, "He esteems his pal with his sugary schlong cravings". I've never known anyone with a sugary schlong, and I hope not to.'

*Daniel Figgis (the artist once known as Binttii),* Hot Press *(9 February 1989)*

'We get a lot of nutty mail. I don't want to exaggerate this, but it is quite worrying. Because of Enya's image she has received a lot of stuff from people who feel they have to protect her from the big bad world and some of them are total lunatics. They start this poetry business and it's obvious that some of them are really disturbed. Now, I'd have to say that Enya would prefer if I played this down, but some of the letters I've seen display a level of almost insane fanaticism which could be dangerous. I suppose all artists get this but the fact of the matter is that some of it is very weird.'

*Nicky Ryan, Enya's manager,* Hot Press *(27 July 1989)*

'Elvis is dead. Now I take over.'

*Aidan Walsh,* Hot Press *(28 January 1988)*

'In the Outer Limits explored by rare, weird, wonderful and terrible beings like The Legendary Stardust Cowboy, Wild Man Fischer and The Bogmen, there too the uncaged spirit of Aidan Walsh swoops and soars like a majestic golden eagle on its way to the labour exchange.'

*Declan Lynch,* Hot Press *(9 April 1987)*

'Rather than being sectioned I went into the loony bin of my own accord. I saw people being given ECT and I saw what it did to them. I saw lots of horrible things, but the minute I was threatened with ECT, I shaped up really fast and became ultra-sane. I started psychoanalyzing my shrink, which was probably part of his technique. He could have sectioned me for another six months but our conversations convinced him of my sanity.'

*Shane MacGowan,* Mojo *(September 2004)*

'You'd be barred from making love in the Underwater City. We'd be very strict on that, to keep the numbers

down. If you come to the city you never die. You'd be
2,000 years old and you wouldn't know it. When the world
blows up, the Underwater City becomes a flying saucer and
leaves the earth. We'd be able to float around for 40 million
years. There'd be about 3 million people in the flying
saucer – it'd be a big one. There'd be two of everything –
two guards, two priests, two doctors. Animals? We might
have one or two. And I'd be the master of it. Master of the
Universe.'

*Aidan Walsh,* Hot Press *(9 April 1987)*


'Every time I offered to beat myself with the beer tray,
Spider [Stacey, The Pogues tin whistle player] said, "No.
I'll do it." That was what was great about him, he had the
guts to beat himself shitless with it every night.'

*Shane MacGowan,* Mojo *(September 2004)*

# DISPUTES

So you think all the boys and girls of the Irish rock scene are friends? You think they live in each others' pockets, houses, gardens, sheds, moored yachts, South of France cottages, Manhattan apartments, backstage green rooms, chartered private jets? You think they're pally-wally all year round, sending each other birthday cards, Christmas cards, swapping prezzies, drinking mulled wine in December and joking with each other whenever they happen to stand under the mistletoe together? We don't wish to come over all cute and red-top tabloid here, but you've really got to think again about this. Some rock stars can't stand the sight of each other (some rock stars can't stand the sight of themselves, but that's another story altogether) and can't wait to shoot off at the mouth about one of their so-called brethren. So let's light the fuse, retreat to a safe distance and watch the sparks fly. (And if you ever call me a little Klimt-viewing, Proust-reading, Truffaut-watching, Rodin-stroking, Stockhausen-listening lover of the German word for art ever again I will have no other option but to request my solicitor to send you a sternly worded letter. So there!)

❖

'I do get a little sick of the self-importance, as I see it. To be honest I wasn't going to say nothing until I saw him kissing the rosary beads that the Pope gave him. Look, he's a good guy and I know he's coming from his heart and so I'm a bitch to even say it, but the one thing that I will complain about is that he put those rosary beads on that microphone [stand] the day the Pope died and went on about how great Catholicism is. I think he should apologise for that.'

*Sinéad O'Connor speaking about Bono,* Mojo *(October 2005)*

'I'm sure they're lovely girls, but they're too skiddely-eye for my liking. Mark my words, they'll do nothing in America. Americans like their music raw. Look at Pearl Jam, Bush. Even the women – Courtney, Sheryl – have a roughness to them. The Corrs are too polished, they're nothing like us. America loves us.'

*Dolores O'Riordan,* Q *(April, 1999)*

'I heard some things. I read another interview where she said something very egocentric. It's a challenge. We won't change our sound and be raw like she says. We'll just be ourselves and see.'

*Andrea Corr replies to Dolores O'Riordan,* Q *(July, 1999)*

'I imagine that Van [Morrison] lives a lot of his life under pressure in his own mind, and gets lots of strange ideas about people.'

*Paul Brady,* Hot Press *(18 June 1987)*

'One time we went to an awards ceremony in Belfast and I was in a lift when three big heavies got in and kicked me out. Then Ronan Keating got in with them and went up, ignoring me and leaving me stranded, so we started dissing him. And then he came up to us when we were in Dublin and asked us why Rick was calling him a cunt. And we said it wasn't Rick it was all of us, and he left looking really flustered. And then he took to kissing his teeth at us whenever we walked past. Oooh, tough guy.'

*Ash's Tim Wheeler and (former member) Charlotte Hatherly,* Q *(October 2002)*

'Cyclops fag! Tried to hit me with a chair once! Grateful for the opportunity to release One By One, but beyond that . . . never seen eye to eye, so to speak! He makes more money than I do, off compilation royalties using Ruefrex songs!'

*Ruefrex drummer Paul Burgess on Good Vibrations label boss Terri Hooley.* It Makes You Want To Spit *(Reekus Music 2003)*

'I think women are supposed to be the fairer sex, more gentle; they don't hassle as much. They are more open and easier to talk to. I don't think I'm rude. Is this an interview or a public hanging? No comment.'

*Van Morrison on being asked why he is so rude to men yet so friendly to women,* Q *(August 1993)*

'For months [Bono] had been uptight about everything, including the music being played behind him. He'd turn and glare at Larry, Edge or Adam if a drum pattern changed or a guitar deviated from the line . . . Towards the end of the gig Larry's snare stand broke. All Bono knew was that Larry had stopped playing. He forgot about audience and performance and turned, enraged, to find Larry grinning sheepishly. Bono charged, hurling his awkward bulk at the drummer, who took evasive action by jumping off backstage. Bono kicked the drum kit over. As it crashed around the stage the audience roared approval. They thought this was part of the show. Bono ran after Larry. As he got to the rim of the stage Edge reached out and grabbed him by the hair. The guitarist rarely lost his cool, but now the Welsh passion so slowly roused boiled over and raged at Bono. Edge wanted to kick the singer's head in.'

*Description of a gig at Toad's Place, New Haven, Connecticut, 15 November 1981 (Unforgettable Fire – the Story of U2 by Eamon Dunphy, 1987)*

'Edge smacked me. It was actually a full-on rumble with all members of the band whacking at me and me whacking at them. It was pure pantomime . . . But Edge packs a punch. There's a lesson here: never pick a fight with a man who earns his living from hand-to-eye co-ordination.'

*Bono recalling the New Haven incident, U2 by U2 (October 2006)*

'Bono could be unpredictable, back then he was always ready for a scrap. He was a terrier and had no fear, you always had that in the back of your mind. No matter how upset you became with him, the only way to deal with it was to run for your life.'

*Larry Mullen Jr's recollection of the same incident,* U2 by U2 *(October 2006)*

'I was ruthless. I talked about the government, the Church, and all the country's ills. I had my dad in my sights. I knew he was watching it down in the boat club. The audience were booing me and everything and the next day at Glasthule church, my father was there and the priest said in his sermon, "Now we're going to say a prayer for that poor demented soul who was on *The Late Late Show* last night and his father is with us today. It must be terrible for him". I learnt later that RTÉ wiped the tape but I know somebody, somewhere has an audio of it.'

*Bob Geldof on his infamous appearance on* The Late Late Show *in the late 1970s,* The Irish Times *(October 2003)*

'He is entitled to his opinion. Planxty, when the deal was set, were just another Irish folk group. So no record company were going to pay . . . I knew musically that they were an important group and that it was an important development in that whole new awareness of Irish music, started by Sean O'Riada – the post-ceili band attitude to

# Disputes

Irish music . . . But talk to Polydor UK and try to tell them that. The last thing I want to do is get into a slagging match with Christy Moore. If he has any beef about the recording situation, the contracts or whatever or the auditing of it, he is and always has been welcome to look at the books. This was a deal with Polydor, which is a major record label. I don't think he can claim to have been ripped off. He may reckon in hindsight that the band now seem to have been a significant band at the time and [should] have been on a bigger royalty, but hindsight is an exact science . . . I can tell you that if I had wanted to rip off a band I would not have chosen Planxty. I would have ripped off a band which was selling hundreds of thousands of albums . . . I probably made more [money] on one single by the Bay City Rollers than I did on all the albums by Planxty . . . I am not in the business of ripping people off . . . My reputation in the record business is a healthy one. Christy might want to point the finger at me for his own reasons. I don't know why he's got sour grapes about it but I certainly have a totally clear conscience.'

*Phil Coulter answering criticisms from Irish singer Christy Moore regarding Irish folk group Planxty and their dealings with the Polydor record label,* Hot Press *(24 December, 1983)*

'You get to that point where you are sick of people annoying you. You're talking to a journalist and you know they're not getting the right vibe, because they don't want to. They want you to be an arrogant bitch. You're not being an arrogant bitch and the journalist continues to ask stupid questions. It's a real pain in the arse, especially when it's from a woman, so it's "listen, love, thanks for coming, sorry to waste your time but I could do better things like washing my cat." On that occasion, anything I said, it was [adopts prissy accent], "Could you explain yourself?" She had this weird vibe and kept staring at me in a strange manner. I thought it was a bitchy thing.'

*Dolores O'Riordan recalls walking out of an interview, having been asked why she dyed her hair, Q (May 1996)*

'Let's talk about Dana. I hate her. I hate her voice. I hate her moaning. She's one of those perennially persecuted people. I was listening to her talking and it seemed that every new stage in her life was the worst thing that ever happened to her. Let's not talk about Dana.'

*Deirdre O'Neill [then of The Joys], In Dublin (1 August 1991)*

'This is something that [Van] Morrison does all the time . . . getting people uptight, confrontation test: let's see how they react when I get there . . . When he got there, [photographer] Brian Aris took him into the studio, and I think he was in there for about ten, fifteen minutes, then there was a crash of tripods and the words, "I finished with this fucking posing years ago." He emerged, with Brian Aris trailing behind him. And he said, "I don't want to do this . . . This is not what I do." And then he made the mistake of going a little bit too far with the confrontation and got the finger out – "What I'm paying you for is to say, no, no, no." At that point I lost it a bit and said, "In that case, get yourself a fucking parrot . . . You either accept my advice or you don't, but if you're not going to what is the point in my being here?" So he said, "I'll think about that," and exited stage left with his girlfriend . . . Then about three days later I got a call at home. He said, "I been thinking about what you said . . . I think you know what you're talking about. What do you want me to do?"'

*Music publicist Keith Altham trying to drum up media coverage of Van Morrison's 1978 album* Wavelength, *as quoted in* Can You Feel The Silence? A New Biography of Van Morrison *by Clinton Heylin (Viking Books 2002)*

'We were together writing for ten years. On day two of our university careers we were introduced by a mutual friend. But by last year he was going in a different direction. Musically and personally. We got to the point we couldn't continue . . . Most marriages don't last five years. It just . . . ran out of steam.'

*Gary Lightbody (Snow Patrol) talking about the band's former bass player Mark McClelland,* Q *(April 2007)*

'We are as good at keeping out of each other's way as we are at being together.'

*Paul McGuinness on the U2 work ethic,* The Irish Times Magazine *(25 August 2001)*

'I don't think U2 have walked on anybody or kicked anyone in the balls . . . We may have kicked each other in the balls a few times, but that's another story.'

*Bono,* Propaganda *(1987)*

## Rockaganda

'One bad habit they [Ash] have picked up is feuding with other bands . . . [Rick] McMurray is amused to learn that he has incurred John Lydon's wrath for his insufficiently punk mohican/spectacles combo. Perhaps it's karmic retribution after a year in which recipients of Ash's scorn have included Starsailor, Toploader and Ronan Keating. "We've had a few people coming up saying, Why are you calling us cunts?" says McMurray. "Ronan was very upset." His expression suggests no sleepless nights.'

*Excerpt from* Q *(December 2001)*

'We tend to have [arguments] in a very, very careful way. One of the things about living with the same five people over ten years is that it teaches you to have disagreements very carefully – nobody wants to start discussions by saying "Well, this is my point of view and anyone who wants to disagree with me can fuck off". That would paralyse our operation, so they never start like that.'

*Paul McGuinness,* Propaganda *(1987)*

'A terrible abortion.'

*Irish traditional musician Noel Hill on the music of The Pogues,* BPFO *(BP Fallon Orchestra), RTÉ Radio One (5 September 1985)*

'Noel Hill told me that I was rubbishing Irish folk music by writing obscene, filthy lyrics, so I said I'm just writing in the tradition, which is raunchy and dirty and ballsy and humorous and sad and funny and horrifically realistic –

life is not a little music box, or a little Irish concertina, like the one you play. And basically that was that. We won the argument.'

*Shane MacGowan, recalling the incident,* Mojo *(September 2004)*

'I found Rory [Gallagher] in the changing room and he succeeded in talking about everything except the split. You can't help liking the guy because he's so nice. It wasn't a case of him making no comment. He just smiled at questions. If the fact be known, he will not discuss it because he does not like putting people down . . . Throughout the whole of the evening not a word passed between Rory and the others. The atmosphere was, to say the least, unnatural.'

Melody Maker *journalist Roy Hollingworth on the Taste split, as quoted in* Mojo *(October 1998)*

'There is a Van Morrison story for every day of the year. Here's another one. A musician who once played in his band recalls an all-night bar-stool debate with the great man. Morrison argued his case, an obscure philosophical point of some sort, with rising force and passion. Worn down and weary, the musician finally conceded defeat. "I agree with you, Van," he said.

"You what?" demanded Van, momentarily thrown.

"What you said, I agree with it."

"Well, in that case," the singer retorts, confidence returning, "in that case, you're wrong".'

Q *magazine (April 1997)*

'I realise that you are claiming you had nothing to do with the publicity which arose concerning you and I in the last few days since the beautiful photos of Frank and myself appeared in the *Mail*. And indeed laughably, you are claiming you don't know why I am at war with you. And that you don't want to be at war with me. It must have been April fool's day yesterday, since you can only have been joking with those two claims . . .

'You know very well that you had agents of yours give interviews to various papers and that you also spoke yourself to various papers wherein they made it seem as if it had been 'a close friend' who spoke. These are facts which I will prove against you in court, should we end up in a court situation . . .

'Be aware, Mary, that I am not the one here who has anything to lose. I have already dealt with twenty-four years of negative publicity and I have no fear of it. Nor any care for what anyone thinks of me. In short, I have nothing to lose from anything that you may think will hurt me so don't think I give a toss what you put in the public arena. This is amusing to me. You are the person here who has more to lose, so I would advise you to back off it now . . .

'I repeat that should we end up in court, you and not I are the one who will suffer most. And should you continue to spread slander against me and pretend it wasn't you who did so, you will regret it in court . . . If I sue you, yes it will be Frank's money I win, as you have so gleefully pointed out. But I will give it straight back to him. And the media will have a field day with you, not me. I do not mind how long it takes Mary . . . I will have you crying for your mummy by the time I have finished with you, and I have nothing whatsoever to lose by taking you on.'

*Excerpts from a letter to Irish singer Mary Coughlan from Sinéad O'Connor, from O'Connor's website (April 2006)*

'We'd appreciate the sales, especially if they were to do it in the first week of release. We had a go at them because they're so embarrassing for Irish music. I can't believe that when you go to Dublin airport there's a huge billboard saying, Welcome to the home of Westlife, so we had a pop at them by burning their albums. And I always make a big point of spitting at that billboard whenever we walk past. They said we couldn't sell 250 records and then we came out with a platinum album, *Free All Angels*, that went to Number 1.'

*Ash's Tim Wheeler on being asked how he would feel if Westlife were to burn 100 copies of an Ash album, Q (October, 2002)*

'The relationship between Feargal and the rest of us – particularly John, who was the leader – worsened. I remember John trying to get him to listen to Al Green, and Feargal refused. Ironic when you think of some of Feargal's solo stuff.'

*The Undertones' Damien O'Neill, Mojo (September 2000)*

'The gig surrounding the incident at the Mansion House supporting SLF was a bit special. Our behavior led us to being corralled off from the others for the rest of the tour!

# Rockaganda

Jake [Burns, Stiff Little Fingers' lead singer] was a fully-fledged legend in his own head by then and the band was becoming very muso. We, with the innocence of part-timers, honestly believed we were flying the flag for punk rock! Food fights backstage; annihilation of all the drink provided by the promoters; baiting of an already hostile audience leading to the toppling of huge PA stacks into the crowd; the wanton destruction [of a hotel] – burning chairs in the lobby; a sea of broken glass in the bar; soap powder in the ornamental water fountain; skinning up joints in the restaurant . . . SLF never talked to us again!'

*Ruefrex drummer Paul Burgess on playing support to Stiff Little Fingers,* It Makes You Want To Spit *(Reekus Music 2003)*

'Dissing the Pope on TV, ripping up a picture of him, claiming you're a lesbian and then that you're not: were you ever an attention-seeker at school?'

'Fuck off.'

*Sinéad O'Connor's pithy reply to a letter from Nuwan Perera, Albuquerque, USA,* Q *(November, 2000)*

'I'm surprised Bono can still talk, his mouth is so full of American politician cock.'

*Sinéad O'Connor,* Q *(January 2006) (Bono's response: 'A mouth full of cock is a tough charge but I can't say I've never felt that myself sometimes.')*

# CRITICS/MEDIA

Happy bedfellows? Don't think so. Quite a number of musicians/creative types would contend that music journalists are frustrated and embittered people who have given up trying to be musicians/creative types because they just didn't have the talent/the luck/the management, etc. And so they do the next best thing: they write about the musicians and creative types they left behind all those years ago. Other musicians/creative types are of the opinion that one of the reasons why music journalists are occasionally so harsh towards particular music acts is that they are jealous of the amounts of money made by people who are (the theory goes) so clearly bereft of true creative talent. Bob Geldof, who knows a thing or two about such matters, reckons that the media as an entity is the single most anti-democratic force in society. There may or may not be a grain of truth in these contentions and opinions, so to refute such accusations would be pointless. All we will say is that there is a place for constructive criticism in all forms of art, of which rock/pop music is one. Is it right to take a pop at buffoons who are perched on their high horses? Is it

morally correct to shoot arrows into the hearts of people
that are clearly – not to put too fine a point on it – so far
up their own arses they can wave at us through their
mouths? Van Morrison says not ('they want to make
themselves look better, or more intellectual'); Paul
McGuinness says yes ('I'm certainly not one of those people
who say that critics don't matter.') Over to you.

'From a band with the ethical sense that U2 has had from
the beginning, we have the right to hear that they have
failed. The market allows them to conceal this. Each year,
each record, a new audience discovers them, and is
infatuated with the wonder of what they represent(ed)
But for those who have been there for a while, never
mind the beginning, there is little left but the wonder of
their survival and their phenomenality.'

*John Waters,* The Irish Book Review *(Autumn/Winter, 2006)*

'Aryan Mist? Rave On, John Donne? Haunts of Ancient
Peace? Listen, I like country walks and metaphysical poetry
as much as the next fellow, but I don't need to hear them
eulogized by the bald, bloated equivalent of a breathless
sixth-form blue-stocking. Van's set-text take on old Albion
is so gauche and jejeune it makes me wince. Worse than
that, his endless accounts of wandering through wet gardens
are just so ploddingly soporific – and rendered in a voice
that's degenerated into a horribly clogged parody of the
supernatural instrument of "Ballerina" or "Into the Mystic"
. . . I don't even mind that it's hard to equate "spirituality"

with someone who so transparently hates himself – that Morrison is merely an old misery-guts crying out for some love and affection while making it impossible for anyone to give it to him . . . I'm afraid I gave up on Van after that cutesy turn with old Cliff, left him to the luvvies and dinner-party bores who will always save room for him in their car stereo . . . For them as for so many people, he remains some kind of Holy Man, albeit a painstakingly grouchy one: a seer who stands alone against the careerist materialism they themselves exemplify. Doubtless his Sacred Cow status has something to do with his Irishness, since that rain-lashed isle continues to serve as an all-purpose "lost home" for rock consumers at large. For me, he's just the saddest old dinosaur in the park.'

*Barney Hoskyns,* Mojo *(November 1993)*

'There are the people who write these so-called biographical books, who haven't done the research, and don't know enough about me in the first place. I think the guys who wrote the last couple of books were complete ignoramuses, not qualified for the job. If anybody told them anything, they believed it, they didn't question it. A lot of the stuff that's been written about me has come from people from thirty or forty years ago, who didn't really know me then, but who have some kind of agenda of their own. They didn't make it, so now they want to get their name in a book. They'll say anything. Some of them, their mental state is quite questionable. I'd go so far as to say that some of the people who talk about me are actually mentally unstable. But the authors don't mention that in their books.'

*Van Morrison,* Mojo *(April 2006)*

'We remember who stood by us back then and had faith in us, that's when we really needed the help and we'll never forget that. We also remember the people who didn't like us back then and now pretend to love us, just because we're successful. We remember everything.'

*Dolores O'Riordan,* The Irish Times *(September 1994)*

'What's the point in having the media there if you don't manipulate them? Their object is to manipulate you in order to get sales. Their sole objective in talking to you is to make money. Journalists get paid and publishers make their wage, either out of advertising or out of the popularity of an artist. They are there, they believe, to manipulate you . . . I've no time for the media at all. They lie most of the time. The same week I appeared in *Marxism Today* and the *Spectator*. Across that broad spectrum of political thought I could read about myself from different editorial viewpoints and each one twisted what I said to suit their own needs. I've also taken part in nearly every accepted media situation, from being in a pop concert to being on the front line of a war and, at all points, I've seen journalists invent stories among themselves. And I'm talking about big opinion-makers, in America and Britain. I've been aware of how newspapers operate since I worked as a journalist in the early '70s, but only now do I really think that the media is the single most anti-democratic force in society ... Even in Africa, journalists twisted the truth. Often to my benefit, I hasten to add. But that's not the point.'

*Bob Geldof,* Hot Press *(December, 1989)*

'The media can say anything about anyone at any time. They can fucking dump on anybody. But if someone like me comes out a nd writes a song that says, "That's not how it is," I get annihilated for it. All hell comes down on me. Well, I've got the freedom to say "Fuck you!", haven't I? That's what these songs are about. I've got my freedom of speech and I'm saying, "Fuck you!" That's it ... If I read a biography about me and I think it's full of bullshit and lies, I've got the right to say that the guy who wrote it is a complete cunt. Is this free country or what?'

*Van Morrison,* Uncut *(July 2005)*

'The British music press ... I hate them, they always mis-quote me and try to make out I'm aggressive or something I'm not.'

*Enya,* Hot Press *(27 July 1989)*

'I don't want some kid across the street shouting at me, calling me names and swearing at me. I work hard, I want a little bit of respect for what I do, but so long as they don't disrespect my family they can say what they want about me. They can all slag, but if I sell records and the fans like what I'm doing, then who are we fooling, man? When people come up and say "Father & Son" or "When You

Say Nothing At All" were played at their wedding, it means so much. That's brilliant, that's respect, that's cool and that's better than any of these other idiots going on about credibility. Pop music is short for popular, that's what it's all about. If you happen to end up credible, so be it.'

*Ronan Keating,* Q *(September, 2000)*

'I don't like them fucking with me. I don't believe in letting people treat you like shit without standing up and saying something about it . . . To me, it's worth it [paying money for a full-page advert in Irish newspapers] because what happens is they've said x, or z about you and then won't print your right of reply. And so, right, fuck yous, I'll buy a fucking page and you'll print my right of reply.'

*Sinéad O'Connor,* Mojo *(October 2005)*

'The media think that we're five guys who, in between robbing cars and living in slums, make records that are fairly good. No one ever questioned where Hothouse Flowers came from, but it was always an issue with us. That was partially our own fault, in that we wanted to celebrate the joys of working-class Ireland. That was turned into what's just been mentioned – we're the scumbags who make music.'

*Aslan's Christy Dignam,* D'Side *(August/September 1994)*

'Some journalists are a real pain in the arse. They go in with an angle and they're going to get you to say what they want you to say somehow, and it's like a battle between you. You're not going to say it and they want you to say it. Then there's others who try to put a really intellectual emphasis on it.'

*Shane MacGowan, Q (December 1994)*

'You can leave a bad impression on people when they see you getting positive press and magazine covers very soon,' he says, 'because if you haven't got the songs to back the coverage they can always turn around and say I told you so. Even if you make a good record, it's not enough for some people. So yes, success might have seemed quick for us, but don't forget we've been playing in one band or another since we were 16. In some people's eyes we haven't paid our dues, but we've been through it all, the record deals, the usual music industry crap. What we hadn't done was to play the Irish circuit, build up a local following, do the local hero thing.'

*The Thrills' Conor Deasy, The Irish Times (September 2004)*

'*Pravda* and the *Skibereen Eagle*.'

*Rory Gallagher's favourite newspapers, Hot Press (22 July 1983)*

'Is it OK if I go to sleep? This is the exact same question . . . Can we have another question? Everybody asks the same first question, the same second question. I'm gonna fall asleep. Can we have something else please? Anything. Anything different.'

*Van Morrison making life difficult for journalist Liam Mackey, Hot Press (October 1988)*

'[Words such as] "Irishness and independence", "spirituality", "community" and "imagination" are always good for a giggle when you wonder just what Bono's lyrics would have been like had it not been for the blokes who wrote the Bible.'

*George Byrne,* Irish Independent *(27 May 2006)*

'Four little leprechauns from Ireland wearing green hats with bows on the tops, who don't have a clue.'

*The Cranberries describing themselves,* Melody Maker *(November 1991)*

'Never liked them [U2]. That whole thing of Bono becoming the Pope – what the fuck's that all about? Pseudo-American rubbish.'

*Paul Weller,* Daily Mail *(May 2006)*

'I've just never been into interviews and I never will be. It's in the music or it's in the songs, so why should I have to explain it? If I thought it would make a difference, then I would probably do more. The propaganda that they put out is that he doesn't do interviews. But I've done loads. We've got press cuttings from here to eternity, and it's never done me any good to do them, ever. It's never changed anything; it's never gotten a different message across. It's never gotten any truth across . . . My interviews work against me because they always come along and say, well, you said this . . . And I might change my mind in a month, so I don't want to be held to some concrete idea that what I'm saying is, like, the law or something and I have to live by that . . . I turn around and get something completely crappy written about me. One asshole in *Rolling Stone* would destroy the whole purpose, so after doing all that work, you still get some guy who will look up the file and go, Van Morrison, he's moody, he's difficult . . .'

*Van Morrison, Q (August 1993)*

'The reason I despise them and hate them [U2] is because of the lies and rubbish they propagate about Ireland and the out-and-out British-supporting propaganda that they put forward around the world. The idea of some major rock star going around the world with a white flag in his hand and singing "Sunday Bloody Sunday" and then saying, This is not a rebel song, has some nerve, as far as I'm concerned, to exploit the pain and suffering of people in a part of . . . whether its his own country or anybody else's. That's the problem I have with them.'

*Fachtna O'Ceallaigh, U2: At the End of the World by Bill Flanagan (Bantam Press 1995)*

'It's typical of the national media – they rarely give coverage to anything or anyone outside Dublin and when they do they get the names wrong. The same goes for bands – no matter how much time, energy and work you put into a gig, you don't get any recognition unless you're from Dublin. It really galls me that bands have to go up to the big smoke to do the business. We did a gig in Leisureland [Galway] recently which attracted 1,500 people and it went totally unmentioned, yet every crappy little band who does ten minutes in The Underground [Dublin] is tipped as the Next Big Thing.'

*Steve Wall (of The Stunning/The Walls),* Hot Press *(11 August 1988)*

'Revealing things about yourself? Well, I think culture in general has accepted that it's okay to ask personal questions. I don't blame the media for that, I blame us as consumers; it's obviously what we're asking for. That said, I refuse to accept that we want to know about Paris Hilton getting out of jail. That's breaking news on Sky? I'm sorry, but I do think we're smarter than that, and I have a far higher regard for people's intelligence.'

*Andrea Corr,* The Irish Times *(December 2007)*

'They [U2] could never fool me! We always had to see over and over again on any television channel that shithead climbing up and down the PA at Redrocks! That guy with the bubble butt waving a white flag! . . . And Edge doing that fucking fake-ass pilgrim gig like, "I'm so pious and low key with my millions . . ." They've been milking that same bassline and the same guitar change for like five albums . . . The world kisses their ass and it is the biggest pile of shite I have ever heard.'

*Henry Rollins,* U2: At the End of the World, *by Bill Flanagan (Bantam Press 1995)*

'Press doesn't sell records or get you fans, it just makes you an icon . . . If you're on a lot of front covers, it just wears

out the name of the band. The art becomes irrelevant.'
*Dolores O'Riordan, Q (October 1994)*

'The most boring band in the world. There may be groups equally as dull, but I fail to see how any of them can be worse.'
*David Quantick on U2, NME (November 1984)*

'If you're talking about music, I think a lot of the people who know most about music are critics. And there are many critics that I have a lot of time for . . . I'm certainly not one of those people who say that critics don't matter. Critics keep you sharp, I think.'
*Paul McGuinness, Hot Press (4 October 2006)*

'They make it more than it is . . . They blow it up out of all proportion, the reason being that they want to make themselves look better, or more intellectual.'
*Van Morrison, Q (April 1997)*

# REVIEWS (BEST)

One person's opinion can, if constructed and directed properly, persuade a reader of a newspaper or a magazine to go out and buy a record. Yet the key words are 'one person's opinion.' It is often the bane of a musician's life that one lone music writer can, with a few (hopefully) well-chosen words, determine the reception of their record. Musicians regularly claim that they don't read reviews of their records, but it surely takes a will of steel not to (and if they don't read the reviews, you can bet someone on their management team does). They also claim that they don't care what anyone says about their work, but, frankly, we're not so sure of that. What we are fairly sure of is that it's always a pleasure to meet a music act that you have given a good review to; they greet you with a hail-fellow-well-met tap on the shoulder or a sturdy shake of the hand, and an offer of a shared alcoholic beverage. For a brief moment in time they are your buddy; you talk about important things such as life, family and art; you part on the best of terms, safe in the knowledge that you'll probably never meet each other again. You really liked their latest album, though; you gave it a glowing review (although you weren't too happy with track number 7), and when news of their forthcoming album filters through the grapevine, you genuinely can't wait to hear it. And when you do eventually get to hear it, via an advance copy of it handed to you personally by the band's manager . . .

'If Thomas Walsh was English he'd be hailed as one of our greatest pop songwriters. Pugwash? Better than McCartney, fatter than Lennon.'

*Andy Partridge of UK powerpop band, XTC, Pugwash press release (16 February 2006)*

'*The Joshua Tree* finally confirms on record what this band has been slowly asserting for three years now on stage: U2 is what the Rolling Stones ceased being years ago — the greatest rock 'n' roll band in the world.'

*Review of* The Joshua Tree, *LA Times (1987)*

'What *Astral Weeks* deals in are not facts but truths. *Astral Weeks*, insofar as it can be pinned down, is a record about people stunned by life, completely overwhelmed, stalled in their skins, their ages and selves, paralysed by the enormity of what in one moment of vision they can comprehend. It is a precious and terrible gift, born of a terrible truth, because what they see is both infinitely beautiful and terminally horrifying: the unlimited human ability to create or destroy, according to whim. It's no Eastern mystic or psychedelic vision of the emerald beyond, nor is it some Baudelairian perception of the beauty of sleaze and grotesquerie. Maybe what it boils down to is one moment's knowledge of the miracle of life, with its inevitable concomitant, a vertiginous glimpse of the capacity to be hurt, and the capability to inflict that hurt.'

*Lester Bangs,* Psychotic Reactions and Carburetor Dung *(William Heinemann 1988)*

'Mary Coughlan never quite fitted. The reasons are many but the basic truth is that her talents weren't slimline and easily stylized. Mythmakers saw only the gardenia in Billie Holiday's hair and forgot Lady Day was originally a country girl. A decade ago, *The Face* promoted Sade as the ideal, and jazz torch singers got stereotyped as vampish urban sophisticates, a process that didn't help Coughlan, whose art concerns kitchen-sink dramas as much as supperclub seduction. It wasn't just a superficial problem of image but a basic difference of attitude. Coughlan empowered women and threatened all those men who only wanted to be flattered. But her originality was also musically confounding since her treatment of jazz and blues was always tinged by her Galway background. Mary Coughlan might cite Billie Holiday as her primary inspiration but she was also an artistic cousin of Dolores Keane, and her blues were always green.'

*Review of* Love Me or Leave Me – the Best of Mary Coughlan, Hot Press *(23 February 1994)*

# Reviews (Best)

'Is *The Joshua Tree* their best record? I wouldn't say that. Some aspects of *Achtung Baby* are as strong, some things in *The Unforgettable Fire* are as touching. It's kind of all a blur to me – maybe it's the drugs!'

*Daniel Lanois,* Mojo *(January 2008)*

'[Van] Morrison has often sounded more intense but seldom as intimate as he does in *Avalon Sunset*: the mystical old croker's capacity to re-work old ground without repeating himself shows no sign of deserting him. And R&B played like this has no sell-by date.'

*From the 50 Best Albums of 1989 List,* Q *(January 1990)*

'There's probably more of Ireland in this record than any LP that's been made here in the last ten years. What other songwriter, for example, would attempt to rhyme "Dia is Mhuire dhiabh" with "the Queen out on a drive" . . . or even mention something like "the children's allowance", for that matter? Joyce with a voice, Yeats on skates or Brendan Behan with an electric guitar, Pierce Turner is a great artist and this could well be his masterpiece.'

*Liam Fay reviewing Pierce Turner's* The Sky and the Ground, Hot Press *(9 February 1989)*

'U2 are the most important band in the history of popular music – about ten million leagues ahead of anyone else, past or present. Sometimes it seems like they exist to show just how mediocre everything else has been.'

*John Waters,* In Dublin *(25 June 1987)*

'*The Joshua Tree* rescues rock from its decay, bravely and unashamedly basing itself in the mainstream before very cleverly lifting off into several higher dimensions. They've been misunderstood occasionally, even by their committed supporters – but after *The Joshua Tree*, with its skill, and the diversity of issues it touches, one thing is absolutely clear: U2 can no longer be patronised with faint and glib praise. They must be taken very seriously indeed after this revaluation of rock.'

*Bill Graham,* Hot Press *(February 1987)*

'It's doubtful such a whimsical non-conformist will fit into the mainstream, but if he can hone his talent and weed out the smartass tendency he could carve himself a niche as a rock literary turn.'

*Divine Comedy's Liberation review,* Q *(October 1993)*

'[*Astral Weeks* is] still the most adventurous record made in the rock medium, and there hasn't been a record with that amount of daring made since.'

*Elvis Costello, as quoted in* Can You Feel The Silence? A New Biography of Van Morrison *by Clinton Heylin (Viking Books 2002)*

# Reviews (Best)

'*The Joshua Tree* is as close to a perfect statement of where rock 'n' roll is at after over thirty years as anyone could wish to send to their relatives on Mars. It is a sign of hope, of redemption, in the barren desert which rock music has become: U2 have assimilated, refined, filtered the language of rock and distilled it into a piece of crystal.'
*John Waters,* In Dublin *(25 June 1987)*

'[*Isn't Anything*] is, according to your taste, either unbearable or truly brilliant. Transfused with energy, eroticism and opacity, the effect ranges from glimmering whispers out of the depths of sleep to twenty-five drunk guitars fucking.'
*Helena Mulkearns on My Bloody Valentine,* Hot Press *(24 August 1989)*

'They're flash and almost chillingly professional, but they do appear to be enjoying themselves again, and there are moments tonight when they're nothing short of excellent. Write them off at your peril.'
*Review of the U2's* Pop *tour date in London's Wembley Stadium,* Mojo *(October 1997)*

'The point of U2 is that they unshakably believe that someone must still fight for that vast, unclaimed territory of popular culture between George Bush and the hardcore, lest nothing be heard beyond the hissing of summer lawns and Whitney Houston albums. But if they double-back, as they regularly do towards the close of *Rattle and Hum*, it's to escape the triple demons of pastiche, dogma and any form of renewed rock tribalism. And yes, of course, *Rattle and Hum* is populist, a stance highly unfashionable among those who fastidiously despair of popular culture, who, in their secret treason see the only useful remaining creative activity as the preserve of those marginalized dandies of the soul who refine emotions and experiences untranslatable to the public arena.'

*Excerpt from review of* Rattle and Hum, *by Bill Graham,* Hot Press *(20 October 1988)*

# REVIEWS (WORST)

. . . it turns out to be a dog's dinner. As we have said, one person's opinion can, if constructed and directed properly, persuade a reader of a newspaper or a magazine to go out and buy a record. Or not. Cue no more hail–fellow–well-met taps on shoulders, sturdy shakes of hands or offers of shared alcoholic beverages. Cue instead withering, how-could-you-betray-me looks at some gig or other. A lifetime of indifference towards you begins.

'It's impossible to take U2 as seriously as they take themselves. When Bono emotes lines like "No one is blinder than he who will not see . . ." I want to wish him a speedy recovery from adolescence.'
*Review of* October, Rolling Stone *(1981)*

'They are as sexy as your least favourite root vegetable . . . and Dolores O'Riordan sings as if for some peculiar ritualistic reason she has placed a selection of marbles in her mouth.'
*Review of* No Need to Argue, Q *(November 1994)*

# Rockaganda

'The Corrs are far from dim; their manager says their next LP "will be their *Joshua Tree*", a plumbing of the soul, and it's not impossible. For now, though, their songs are sugar-coated pop with a touch of Celtic lilt, and they stick like candyfloss, like the croons of Tribbles.'

*Review of show at Wembley Arena, London,* Mojo *(March 1999)*

'Another example of rock music's impotence and decay.'

*Review of U2 album* War, NME *(March 1983)*

'The real problem with it is that it starts from the basic concept that U2 are somehow a cultural force rather than a reasonably good rock singles band with a nifty guitarist and an extremely astute manager.'

*George Byrne, reviewing the book* U2, an Irish Phenomenon, *by Visnja Cogan,* Irish Independent *(27 May 2006)*

'Just one of the dough-faced Post Office advertisers' crimes against the rhythmic vibrations of air molecules.'

*Review of Westlife's single, "Seasons In The Sun",* The Word *(April 2008)*

'With few exceptions, this is Caledonian Soul with a full bib and tucker, the stilted musical equivalent of an awards ceremony.'

*Review of tribute album,* No Prima Donna – the Songs of Van Morrison, Q *(August 1994)*

'I thought of *Zooropa* at the time as a work of genius. I really thought our pop discipline was matching our experimentation and this was our Sergeant Pepper. I was a little wrong about that . . .'

*Bono,* U2 By U2 *(October 2006)*

'A cross between The Bangles and The Nolans. That may be enough to shift multi-platinum quantities in America from now until doomsday but it's unlikely to stand up to repeated plays if you like a bit of meat on your bone.'

*From review of The Corrs album* Forgiven Not Forgotten, Q *(May 1996)*

'Somewhere in the mid-eighties the poet/philosopher accolades seem to have seeped into his skull and he began churning out same-sounding albums on an almost annual basis. Musically, they were largely sub-Mantovani mush, while the lyrics resembled the work of chimpanzees cutting up extracts from Yeats, Hopkins, Blake and Donne, then pasting the resulting mess to the side of a bus shelter.'

*Excerpt from a review of Van Morrison's* Back On Top, *George Byrne,* Irish Independent *(March 1999)*

'There's a rumour going around that Van Morrison has been singing and writing the same song for the past ten years. Listening to his new single – the title track of new album, *The Healing Game* – one is moved to agree. It's the same soul cry for salvation, and the same lyrical repetition, the mantra quality of which is now surely more caricatured than celebrated. The word "jellyroll" is mentioned. You have been warned.'

*Review of 1997's* The Healing Game, In Dublin *(13 February 1997)*

'I am as saddened as anyone by the decline of Ronnie Drew in the face of the merciless onslaught of cancer, but just because this is recorded in his honour and proceeds go to the Irish Cancer Society does not preclude it from criticism. This is unworthy of his name. It's an embarrassingly bad series of contributions from artists who should really have known better. The tune is dreadful, with moon and June-style rhymes from Bono and the likes of Shane MacGowan, Andrea Corr and others in his cosy cabal. Damien Dempsey should certainly know better. And as for Glen Hansard phoning in his contribution . . . How appropriate.'

*Review of* The Ballad of Ronnie Drew, *by U2, Kila, The Dubliners and others,* Irish Mail on Sunday *(24 February 2008)*

'It is with both incredulity and disappointment that I find myself resorting to the pen to sate the anger felt over *The Ballad of Ronnie Drew*, which has just been unleashed on an unsuspecting world. While accepting that the cause may be noble and the sentiment laudable, it cannot excuse this lamentable effort from the supposed cream of the country's musical talent. Rather than the epic which might have been expected, we are subjected to a mish-mash of styles in a formula which has worked only once with Band Aid's "Do They Know It's Christmas". You would have thought that a subject so colourful as Ronnie Drew would provide any lyricist with enough material from which to construct a fitting tribute. But it wasn't enough for Bono and Simon Carmody, who sought the assistance of Robert Hunter from the Grateful Dead (the most boring band in history) The result is awful. Lyrically, it is embarrassing (at best), even though it is propped up with two passages from the traditional standard "Easy And Slow" . . . What has particularly irked, though, are the reactions of some of our best-known personalities like Gerry Ryan, Pat Kenny and Derek Mooney who have been gushing in their praise for this abomination, while *Hot Press* editor Niall Stokes, surely tongue in cheek, has branded it "an astonishing record". Either they aren't prepared to risk incurring the wrath of Bono et al by questioning its merits, or they do not know their arses from their elbows. As for poor Ronnie, hasn't he suffered enough? The least they could do to aid his recovery is remove his name from the title of this abomination.'

*Letter writer Séan De Faoite,* Irish Mail on Sunday *(24 February 2008)*


'A collection of "imagined" movie themes piloted by Eno in full bleepy, wibbly pomp with a bit of Pavarotti thrown in, it makes *Zooropa* sound like the Pussycat Dolls.'

*Review of* Passengers: Original Soundtracks 1, Mojo *(May 2007)*

# ME, MYSELF, I – THE EGO HAS LANDED

You can't scramble eggs without breaking them, and you can't be a musician – a successful one anyway, and all that it entails – without having an ego. Generally, the ego is a large and fragile thing; the sensitivity of some musicians to the reception of their art is often astonishing to behold – indeed, such sensitivity is possibly the reason why they are creative types in the first place. Yet it is when dents to the ego are received with such pained expressions that you start to wonder where exactly the flaws reside – in the critic or the artist?

'Tall, intelligent, modest.'
*Bono on being asked how he was, Q (November 2006)*

'For years people have been saying to me – you know, nudge, nudge – have you heard this guy Springsteen? You should really check him out! I just ignored it. Then four or five months ago I was in Amsterdam, and a friend of mine put on a video. Springsteen came on the video . . . and he's definitely ripped me off . . . I mean, he's even ripped my movements off as well . . .'

*Van Morrison quoted in* Can You Feel The Silence? A New Biography of Van Morrison *by Clinton Heylin (Viking Books 2002)*

'When you're sixteen, you think you can take on the world. And sometimes you're right.'

*Bono,* Achtung Baby: the Videos *(1992)*

'We are a tight family, with all the pluses and disadvantages of that. But we don't have an ego problem in the band. We all are involved in the process. We all struggle together.'

*Larry Mullen Jr,* Sunday Times Magazine *(7 November 2004)*

'There's a skyscraper in Singapore with our faces on the side. We're really big in Israel. I don't know how many we've sold but apparently we're gods.'

*Westlife's Nicky Byrne,* Q *(July 2000)*

'I must say I prefer playing Wembley Arena, I really do, that is no joke. The music never seemed to fit into those places. They always seemed too small . . . We wanted to blow the roof off. I always felt like that. We needed to find a bigger place to play even if there weren't any people there.'

*Bono, when asked did he have a hankering to play small Dublin music venue McGonagles again,* Propaganda *(winter 1988)*

'I know the reason I'll have a Number One in America, and probably will be the biggest thing to come out of Ireland, is because when they put on my record it'll frighten the bloody life of them!'

*Stano, talking about his third album,* Only, *Hot Press (4 May 1989)*

'It's hard to have an ego when you're dealing with prisoners of conscience as an issue.'

*Adam Clayton on the 1986 Conspiracy of Hope tour,* U2 by U2 *(October 2006)*

'I don't mean to sound arrogant, but even at this stage, I do feel that we were meant to be one of the great groups. There's a certain spark, a certain chemistry that was special about the Stones, the Who and the Beatles, and I think it's also special about U2.'

*Bono,* Propaganda *(February 1981)*

'I wasn't helpful to Toasted Heretic. I needed an enormous amount of arrogance just to get up in the morning. I signed on the dole for a decade, and I was doing creative work that I knew was really good. You need an immense level of arrogance when nobody agrees with you, in order to keep going. Of course, that puts a lot of people off, and I can understand that. I don't blame anyone for disregarding us because I happened to shout too loudly on our behalf, but no one else was shouting for us. But I believed in what we did, and I couldn't understand why people couldn't see that there was something to us. We should have been cherished and helped, rather than ignored or sneered at, or put down as "quirky band with an arrogant singer". So I certainly didn't help the band, but the virtues I had meant that we recorded albums when everyone else just listened to them. But, yes, if you could suffer from high self-esteem, then I certainly suffered.'

*Toasted Heretic's lead singer and novelist Julian Gough,* The Irish Times *(November 2005)*

'There's been a suggestion that U2 will react to Zoo TV by doing something plain and simple, but we wouldn't really be interested in that. People always say "Wouldn't it be great to see U2 in a club?", and I have to say to them, "No, it would be terrible." There's no going back . . .'

*Paul McGuinness, as quoted in* In Dublin *(16 January 1997)*

'Everyone says I'm arrogant but I don't think I am.'

*Bob Geldof,* Q *(January 1995)*

'There is something very uncomfortable about a rich rock star being photographed with poor, starving kids. In that sense I wish it wasn't me. I don't blame people for being cynical. I'm sure it's not all altruistic. There must be some

ego involved . . . I have the sort of personality where I
believe I can always find a solution.'
*Bono, Q (November 2004)*

'He's a rampant sex god with a huge ego.'
*Edge on Bono, The Face (April 1992)*

'And a small willy.'
*Adam Clayton adds, The Face (April 1992)*

'I have an ego in certain things. Because I'm self-critical,
because I'm me own worse critic, I know me good
points, so I wouldn't be modest when I know I'm good.'
*Phil Lynott, Hot Press (18 May 1984)*

'People must be so sick of seeing me by now on TV or
reading about me or just constantly being exposed to me.
I thought that after a certain point it just appears normal
that there is this kind of growing media stature, but after
that point it works against itself. I can walk through
Clapham and people just go, "'Ello Bob". If you don't
ponce about in limos . . . I don't make a point of walking
through the fokkin' West End, but if I have to get to the
Marquee I'll take the tube and walk. There are no riots in
the street, but people come up and ask for autographs –
and I wanted that accessibility, so that people wouldn't be
afraid to come up and chat . . . It wasn't any big crusade,
any great plan to demystify as such, I just never saw any
necessity to become a Rod Stewart or a Rolling Stone or

a Beatle. The Beatles probably couldn't go out on the street without being seriously mobbed, but I figured that if I shot my mouth off constantly people would get tired of seeing me . . .'

*Bob Geldof,* NME *(20 October 1979)*

'I hate failing. Hate it. I hate failure.'

*Ronan Keating,* Q *(September 2000)*

# MUSIC INDUSTRY

It's a simple fact: you can't want to be a successful, wealthy musician (or even a working musician, trying to claw your way up from nothing to something) if you don't engage in some shape or form, or on some level, with the music industry. It's a blessing and a curse (although mostly the latter, according to well-placed sources), and it's a necessary evil, but if you don't join the club, even on a trial basis, you'll have a hard time turning into what you think you want to be. No one is saying it's easy having to deal with record companies and their accountants, flow charts and A&R staff. No one is saying it's easy having to do weeks of promotional duties, talking to media people you'd really rather not spend time thinking about let alone being in the company of. And no one is saying that the music industry cares about you any more than you care about it. Ultimately, it's a shared experience, where the aspirations of one rarely match the expectations of the other, where expense accounts are shagged regularly and senselessly, and where promotional T-shirts always seem to outlast the music acts they advertise. Welcome to the machine, an entity where buying the MD a drink helped getting some bands signed, where icons are created and then dropped at the flick of a switch, and where success depends purely on being the right act in the right place at the right time. Hands up who'd rather be a plumber?

'In the old days they [hustlers] were easier to spot because the music business was very small. Now it's become much more like a corporate affair, and it's legitimised. I think there are more hustlers in the music business than in any walk of life. A lot of people in the music business could not exist in another business ... The music business is built as a façade where the non-ethical has become normal and become establishment. It's camouflaged by pseudo-ethics.'

*Van Morrison,* Mojo *(August 1995)*

'I think the only thing that might make me want to stop would be the music business, because for any intelligent, thinking person, the music business is bullshit.'

*Van Morrison – still of a similar opinion,* Mojo *(April 2006)*

'The one thing no one seems to understand about the management business is that it's only a great idea when it works,' says Woods ruefully. 'Other than that, it's all money out and nothing coming in. It's a thankless task; unless you hit paydirt, that is, and then you're Mister Wonderful.'

*Terry Woods,* The Irish Times *(August 2002)*

'We got to the point where we weren't making enough money to pay rent. To be honest, I think the record label lost interest in us. We stumped up the cash to enter ourselves into the Mercury Music Prize because we thought it might generate some interest. We didn't get shortlisted.'

*Gary Lightbody (Snow Patrol), Q (August, 2004)*

'We never had the opportunity to say to our manager we didn't want to do something. One thing you can say about The Pogues was that individually we were very clever but collectively we were very stupid. I remember the manager saying, "lads, give us the next two years of your lives and we'll make successes of you". That turned into four, six, eight years . . . but once your head's jammed so far in the railings, it's hard to get it out.'

*The Pogues' instrumentalist James Fearnley, The Word (January 2005)*

'Scullion are almost terminally uncool. They're hardly a band that you would admit to liking let alone tell someone that you owned one of their records. The attitude of some people is "who the hell do they think they are?" and "why do we need another bunch of old folkies anyway?" When you're up you're up, but when you're down, down you go. The band has always been a commercial dilemma in terms of the way we've related to the music business. We've never been able to find a conduit into that world at all. We've always been too early with something and then other people latched onto it and made a go of it. And I'd have to

admit that we've suffered financially because of our inability to become part of the music industry.'
*Philip King,* Hot Press *(20 October 1988)*

'The fact that I'm forty years old and people still talk about me like I'm some sort of three-year-old. That's wounding to say the least. So much of the industry is based upon bullshit.'
*Sinéad O'Connor,* Uncut *(July 2007)*

'I don't know why people liked [Boyzone], but we were real people. There were no weird attitudes or egos, we were a bunch of lads having a good time and everybody saw that. We were partners in a business arrangement and were lucky that five lads thrown together got on. Louis [Walsh, manager] taught us to be nice to everyone and we picked the right songs. Who cares that they were covers? They were hit records.'
*Ronan Keating,* Q *(September 2000)*

'Anybody who gets involved in the music business and doesn't see it for the devil it is, is a fool. I only discovered it by age; the music business is sickening, it's revolting. A majority of journalists are daft. I have no idea why it exists.'
*Terry Woods, The Pogues,* Hot Press *(28 January 1988)*

'I came over to look at U2 in The Baggot Inn, but got rat-arsed in the Shelbourne Hotel and never made it. The following night I went to see The Lookalikes and signed them rather than waste a trip. Not a great bit of business in retrospect.'

*A&R man Billy Gaff, of then Riva Records. Regrets? He's had a few. As quoted in* In Dublin *(7 November 1996)*

'Y'see, if I were to say to you, "well I sat back last year and I looked at my career and I looked at all the things I can do well . . ." that's what ruined rock 'n' roll. They have board meetings now. The Wall Street mentality's creeping in.'

*Rory Gallagher,* Hot Press *(December 1988)*

'We've been dating for over twenty years now – it's about time we tied the knot.'

*Bono on the signing by U2 of an estimated $300 million-plus, twelve-year contract with Los Angeles-based entertainment company Live Nation,* The Irish Times *(1 April 2008)*

'I'd say most artists would probably feel they got fucked over [by the music industry]. What I feel is you can be fooled into thinking that it gives a shit about you. But they're not necessarily there for you if and when you're in the nuthouse because of the effects of the journey they've brought you on.'

*Sinéad O'Connor,* Mojo *(October 2005)*

'It comes from the top down. Bono has told me that if any big shot who comes backstage ever gives me a bad time I can tell him to fuck off. Do you know what a relief that is? Some people – LA is the worst for this – are so rude, so demanding and ungrateful. They get complimentary tickets and if they see somebody they know with better complimentary tickets they get upset with us. Their prestige is determined by how good their free seats are!'

*Sheila Roche, of Principle Management, U2: At the End of the World, Bill Flanagan (Bantam Press 1995)*

'I can remember when we first signed a record deal. It's such a buzz, so exciting. You're completely taken in by it all. Even if it goes horribly wrong after a few years, it's still a wonderful thing. We, however, would have signed for a fiver, a pint of beer and ten ciggies, because all we wanted to do was to make a record. Nothing more. Thankfully, our manager steered us onto the right path by having good accountants and lawyers. Which you do need, because there's an inordinate amount of money being thrown around. When you subtract all the things that you have to spend money on to survive in the business, it doesn't amount to that much at all. It's important to have someone around who is able to see through the excitement, and to ensure that everything is in order. That you're not signing away anything you don't want to sign away. It doesn't make a lot of difference when you're not making any money, but if/when you do, it makes all the difference in the world.'

*Hinterland's Gerry Leonard, Hot Press (7 April 1993)*

'When people say, you guys are fucking great, there's the ching-ching in their eyes, which means, you guys are going to make me a lot of money.'

*The Cranberries' bassist Mike Hogan, Q (May 1996)*

# Rockaganda

'At first you feel duty-bound to fulfill all these commitments, but they just mounted up until they became completely ridiculous. We stopped doing interviews because we were sick of them, and I started to lose my temper a lot . . . Meanwhile, I'd gone down to six-and-a-half stone, not because I was anorexic or anything, but because I'd stopped eating. My entire diet consisted of cigarettes and coffee. I hadn't slept properly for months and months, and I'd just reached the end. I couldn't take it anymore. I was really quite messed up, an absolute nervous wreck . . . We didn't go mad, as such, but we all had a lot of weird episodes. Noel [Hogan] would go really quiet, and completely withdrawn. But Feargal [Lawler] was hysterical. When he went weird, he'd kick his drum kit black and blue. I remember finishing a concert, and saying to the crowd, thank you, you've been fantastic. But then as I walked off, I'd see Feargal screaming like a madman and kicking the bollocks out of his drums. Then he'd catch my eye, and go running off, suddenly really embarrassed. And when Mike [Hogan] went weird he'd become the absolute lunatic with the drink. Oh Jaysus, he'd drink the bar dry, then climb up onto it and have a little dance. You've not seen Mike dance, have you? He isn't great.'

*Dolores O'Riordan, Q (April 1999)*

'All the people I look after have their own lawyer, they know what they're getting into. I know from watching them if they have a long career or not.'

*Louis Walsh, Cara Magazine (July 2002)*

'Some of the bands we signed up were the worst in the world. It was either because I liked the band members' girlfriends or some other obscure reason. If I liked the band personally, that was half the battle. You didn't have to be a great band to get on the label. There was no format to getting signed. Buying me a drink helped!'

*Terry Hooley, creator of Belfast's Good Vibrations label,* D'Side *(April/May 1994)*

'I was never bothered by their Eurovision video, that was a cheeky scam that thoroughly deserved its success. Rather, was it a case of too much, too soon? Like so many late eighties bands, did the Hothouse Flowers feel forced to prematurely boost their profile before it was creatively justified? Pragmatists who appreciate rock realpolitik will disagree. With the partial exception of hard rock, the global music business is no longer geared to gradual development, to that sort of measured, patient progress where the music can keep pace with the hype. These times, acts are expected to early establish a global brand-name, take the company's money and run, rocking all over the world, schmoozing with every compliant hack who'll buy their press office's sell. Besides, since first album successes are more profitable due to their lower royalty rates, terms like nursery reserve teams and second division acts are increasingly alien to the music business. Perhaps the Flowers had no choice but to paint themselves as stadium stars in waiting. But in the process, the Hothouse Flowers bypassed the Irish rock press crew. Back in '88 they launched themselves and their debut album, *People*, through the features desks of the Irish papers who'd finally copped on to the circulation-building potential of Irish rock and so were entirely willing to hail the Flowers as the next U2. Certainly, they suited the media's specifications for young Irish success stories. Why, they were even Irish speakers . . . But this initial sidelining of the Irish rock press in favour of soft features rebounded on them. It left a residue of scepticism that sometimes bordered on outright suspicion among those who followed their continuing career. And devotional UK press coverage that was close to hagiography, as if the Flowers were the new druids of occidental mysticism, hardly improved local scribes' goodwill. Certainly, I recall one reception when a trio of us entertained ourselves counting the number of times – over 50, in fact – when Liam Ó Maonlaí flicked his locks from over his eyes in the "Don't Go" video. That climate definitely aided the proliferation of Hothouse Flowers' rumours. It was also why they became so identified with That Difficult Second Album.'

*Excerpt from 'The Hothouse Effect' article, Bill Graham,* Hot Press *(15 August 1990)*

'I don't like to think about it because it upsets me. The whole thing has made me very wary of music business people. I don't give a damn about the money – it's people who let you down that bothers me most.'

*Rory Gallagher on the litigation process, as quoted in* Mojo *(October 1998)*

'(Rock) bands . . . have it a million times harder. My brother's in a rock band and he's been slogging around for three years. They go into the studio, record their own stuff, try to get development deals. It's such a different ballgame in the rock world. For us, it either happens for you or it doesn't, simple as that. If it doesn't happen in the first six months . . . you'll probably get dropped.'

*Westlife's Kian Egan,* Q *(July 2000)*

'I went back to them and told them they'd have to give the money because I'd already signed cheques for what I needed. They laughed but they covered the cheques. They view the music business as something they might like to have an association with but they won't get into bed with you. No matter who you are or how successful you are they'll look for back-to-back financing. You've got to find a pound for every pound they loan you.'

*Robbie Wootton, former manager of Hothouse Flowers, on his dealings with banking institutions,* D'Side *(August/September 1994)*

'I loved his music, but I just couldn't [renew] the deal after looking at his sales, and [considering] the fact that you could have no input with the guy at all. He was as difficult as anyone I ever dealt with. He would explode on stage, in your office, having dinner at the house. I remember we almost came to blows because he kept insisting that I guarantee him a number one single . . . I kept saying, "Van, who can guarantee you a hit?"'

*Mo Ostin, one-time President of Warners Record Division, on Van Morrison,* LA Times *(6 June 1996)*

# Rockaganda

'Why spend a lot of money on a video for satellite stations that nobody watches? We're not going to spend £20,000 to get 20,000 viewers. Besides which, when I think of videos I think of Brother Beyond and the like, whereas Something Happens are a sweaty, hairy bunch of sex gods. I'd much rather give them money to tour live rather than spend it on one video which some BBC producer will decide he doesn't like and it doesn't get shown . . . And if Tom [Dunne, Something Happens lead singer] is reading this, tell him I said he's to get his hair cut. He looks like a fucking King Charles spaniel.'

*Ronnie Gurr, former Virgin UK A&R,* Hot Press *(20 April 1989)*

'We had this idea that you should be creative in business, that you didn't have to divide it up into art and commerce. We'd meet these record company people on tour in the US and to most punk bands coming out of the UK, these were the enemy. And I didn't think they were the enemy. I thought they were workers who had gotten into music for probably all the right reasons, and weren't as lucky as we were, weren't able to fulfill their ambition to be musicians and were now working the music. Maybe they lost their love and I felt that part of our thing was to re-ignite that. So a lot of people got inspired and they rallied around us, creating a network, and that protected us, created this kind of cushion. Then you start to see organization in a creative light. You start to say, "Well, these are important decisions, this artwork . . ." And you realise that, in fact, to be a group is the art.'

*Bono,* U2: At the End of the World*, Bill Flanagan (Bantam Press, 1995)*

'There's all these bands like An Emotional Fish and The Fat Lady Sings, trapped by that wonderful record company, trapped like flies in a web. They're choosing singles and videos that they think are commercial and fucking nothing is happening. Once you're honest with yourself and just put out what you want, maybe it'll come through for you.'

*A House singer, Dave Couse,* Hot Press *(12 December 1991)*

'The record company tell you to go out and promote the new album. So I try and sing a new one and now I can't remember the fuckin' words.'

*Christy Moore,* Mojo *(January/February 1994)*

'They're absolute bastards in this business. It's really scary. When it comes to your career, it can be all over in the morning, finished in a heartbeat.'

*Ronan Keating,* Q *(September 2000)*

'The day of major labels is completely finished. Unless you're a priority act, or if there's a buzz about you and you want to have a great time for a year, then you'd be mad to sign to a major label. If you want to seriously sustain or hold any integrity in your life then you should forget about major labels.'

*Marc Carroll,* The Irish Times *(November 2005)*

'Cocaine was everywhere. One of any number of Artie Fufkins would chop out a line and tell you they were going to bust their ass breaking your record in some or other state. And for five minutes, not only did you believe them, but you were whooping along with them. The reality was that you were somewhere in the Midwest working through a schedule that made no sense, with people that didn't know how to pronounce your name. Somewhere at home, I still have a name pass with the words "Brad Gandalf" on it.'

*Bob Geldof on the Boomtown Rats' stab at success in America,* Mojo *(May 2005)*

'Paul McGuinness was an important step, and we went after him in a very determined way . . . We didn't want to be a cult group, we wanted to be a big group and we thought that's where our talents lay, that's what we, as a group of guys together, had the potential to be. We needed Paul McGuinness to help us do that.'

*Edge,* U2 Faraway So Close *(1994)*

'Unless your first album sells absolutely millions and there's a huge amount of pressure to match that then I reckon it's best to follow up a debut really quickly before people forget about you. That whole "one album every three years" scenario seemed daft to us, especially when you look back and realise that there were times when The Beach Boys were releasing three great albums a year and touring their asses off as well.'

*Thrills guitarist Daniel Ryan,* Cara Magazine *(September 2004)*

'Okay, here's the dilemma. You make two albums, you tour your arse off and you hit a wall. Do you finish with the band or take an offer from the one label who were interested in us, who happened to be a major.'

*Gary Lightbody (Snow Patrol),* Q *(August 2004)*

'We seem to have lost our shirts and now they're starting to unravel our string vests. It's an extremely depressing business purely because of the amount of time and energy it saps. There seriously were times when I felt like jacking it all in and doing a runner. I would have had no qualms about doing that if I thought I'd get away with it. I remember one account that was done and it showed that Microdisney had made a total profit of £1 in all our years of existence. Now it looks as if we'll end up owing the government money when everything is balanced out. For a long time I felt like an irrelevancy in an irrelevant situation but as I gradually waded through all this business crap I realised that there was nothing else I could do but form another band.'

*Cathal Coughlan,* Hot Press *(14 June 1990)*

'In certain aspects the band weren't completely honest with me. When I gave them proofs for correction, a lot of the things they corrected were later identified by their friends in the press as false. Now that's a very Machiavellian trip. I don't want to go into it in too great detail . . . but they fucked me . . . It was quite a difficult experience . . . It's a bit disturbing to find that something you've been told isn't true and that you then have to carry the can for that.'

*Writer/broadcaster Eamon Dunphy on his experience of writing U2's official 1987 biography* The Unforgettable Fire, *In Dublin (10 October, 1991)*

'No other band has come anywhere as close to transcending the Music Business's obsessive need to turn musicians into icons.'

*John Waters on U2, In Dublin (25 June 1987)*

'We tried to arrange a meeting with Pearse [Gilmore], so we could discuss the possibility of signing them, because Rob Dickens [Warners MD] liked the tape and we decided it would be a good Blanco y Negro project [Warners subsidiary], but Pearse wouldn't take my calls or set up a business meeting. Which is pretty unusual behaviour for a manager whose group is unsigned. It was very, very odd.'

*Rough Trade boss Geoff Travis on trying to sign up The Cranberries, Q (October 1994)*

'We were hit and miss. We could have three great gigs in a row and then two shite ones – the record companies would always make it to the shite gigs.'
*Larry Mullen Jr, U2 by U2 (October 2006)*

'My experience of an indie label is that, while the passion is there, they're a bit of a madhouse. Sometimes, the passion displayed itself in very peculiar ways that didn't always seem to be to your advantage. With the major label you don't have the same immediacy and hands-on thing – no matter how nice they are, because they have other acts that are very successful and that take up a lot of their time. But the major label gives me money; they give me time, freedom.'
*Neil Hannon (Divine Comedy), Cara Magazine (June 2003)*

'People like Bros – I know it's a horrible thing to say – were kind of guinea pigs for everybody else. They made millions and lost it all. How? Why? And people have learnt from that – Take That, Boyzone, us. We deal with bank managers and accountants and lawyers every second day.'
*Westlife's Nicky Byrne, Q (July 2000)*

'Paul [McGuinness] was not a warm, fuzzy feeling . . . The most striking thing about Paul was:"I don't want to be your friend. I'll be your manager." There was no attempt to play at friendship. Very interesting . . . My old man met Paul. Paul speaks with the low hum of the

British ascendancy, so that means my dad immediately doesn't trust him. He was saying, "Watch that fellah.'"
*Bono,* U2 By U2 *(October 2006)*

'Around 1995 . . . it was more physical fatigue and loss of weight than anything else. Basically, what I wanted was a career break, but a lot of people around me didn't want to hear that. Bands are sometimes the centre of a massive corporate workhorse, and it's not just about your own CDs and how you're doing, but also about how the record company is doing and how their employees depend on you. If you take a break, it filters down to many, many people. I probably wouldn't be here if I hadn't taken that break.'
*Dolores O'Riordan,* Cara Magazine *(March 2002)*

'I'd put a lot of myself into the second Fat Lady Sings album, *Johnson*, emotionally, and in much more practical ways than is normal for people in bands. I felt that the ball was getting dropped in many ways, and I wasn't prepared to let that happen again. But eventually I felt that no matter what I did for *Johnson*, it would never be enough to make the album happen . . . I realised that if the industry structure isn't right, it doesn't matter how hard you work. I have low expectations of other people, which isn't necessarily a bad thing, so I wouldn't assume that someone in record companies would do this right. So I would check on them, again not a bad thing, but it brought home to me that you can't do this by yourself. Everything is a meeting, and everyone is sucked into these ridiculous record company loops by people who are afraid of losing their jobs. After a while you can't even work out whether you believe yourself.'

*Nick Kelly, then lead singer and main songwriter of Fat Lady Sings,* In Dublin *(13 March 1997)*

'It's not about being a sex bomb, but trying to portray an image of today's woman that's strong and a bit different.'

*Róisín Murphy on being a 'woman in rock',* Q *(September 2000)*

'When you are young you don't know you can say no. Around the time of "Nothing Compares To You" I went on tour for nine months, which is absolutely ridiculous. I never did that again. Working with big record companies there is a pressure put on you to produce a hit record. I think I was stunted by this – I couldn't actually make the records I wanted to.'

*Sinéad O'Connor,* Cara Magazine *(October 2002)*

'I've been managing U2 for 30 years. We've made some mistakes but the line-up hasn't changed and the band are as ambitious as ever. U2 own all their masters and copyrights and license them to Universal. We always understood that it would be pathetic to be good at the music and bad at the business. We were never going to be victims.'

*U2 manager Paul McGuinness, from his keynote address (The Online Bonanza: Who is Making the Money and Why Aren't they Sharing it?) at the 42nd edition of Midem, France (28 January 2008)*

# Rockaganda

'Building up America was a mistake, saying I was going there for six months and that I was going to break it. I blame myself for that, but I was excited about it, making the first album out there, thinking I was going to live there. But it's all about radio play, the amount of spins you get – there was so much absolute bollocks to it . . . The Americans totally cut themselves off from the rest of the world. They don't listen to the charts outside their own territory – it is its own world.'

*Ronan Keating,* The Irish Times *Magazine (27 April 2002)*

'You expect them [managers] to be manky, unshaven and wearing a long grey coat, and you expect them to have a big cigar and smiles on their faces. Most managers I've met are frustrated musicians, people who are attracted to the industry because they wanted to be rock stars themselves but didn't have the talent. Aslan have something that is a commercially viable product, let's say, and you have all these people wondering how they're going to get a slice of that without having to create anything. That's fairly across the board in my experience. If we had met the person that isn't the sleazeball, they'd be managing us by now. The thing is, they're not obviously sleazeballs. I suppose it's their job – they have a family to feed as well, and that's their way of doing it. But I didn't look to Michael Smurfit to see how I could get a slice off his sweat. I had to work out myself how to do it, so I don't respect anyone who doesn't do that.'

*Aslan's Christy Dignam,* D'Side *(August/September 1994)*

'The reason they [Thin Lizzy] broke up is that every single band has its moment. For five minutes you're allowed what I call the tee-hee factor, that sneaky tee-hee when you make it on Top of the Pops. Then you almost wish you hadn't made it, because you're standing around in a studio all day with some idiot trying to tell you how to do your song. Once you make it you realise you have a responsibility; the pressure on you becomes unbelievable. Then five years go by in a blink, and suddenly you have promoters, agents, record company and managers telling you that you don't need to do this tour or release that album and you find yourself agreeing. Then you find yourself doing solo work to fill in the time, and you start to hasten your own downfall.'

*Chris O'Donnell, former Thin Lizzy manager,* Mojo *(December 1993)*

# WOMEN AND MEN

Money makes the world go around? Er, no, actually. What makes the world go around is the difference between the sexes. Different viewpoints, different worldviews, different types of responsibilities, different needs, different music. Not always different hairstyles or clothes, but you can't have everything, can you?

'I'm spending Christmas down at Geldof Towers . . . My dad'll be there, drunk on wine, spewing on about the past and singing a couple of Boomtown Rats hits while I cry in the corner. That's what it's like. Every year. Every. Year. You know, my dad is really anal about Father Christmas. We have to be asleep when he brings the stockings in. I woke up last year when he was doing it and I started screaming because I thought he was a psychopath.'

*Peaches Geldof,* NME *(December 2007)*

'People have tried to figure out our marriage for years. It's simple. Relationships need management and she's a very good manager. There's still a lot I don't know about her. She's a mystery to me. Sometimes I feel I'm not good enough for her.'

*Bono talking about his wife, Ali, Q (November 2004)*

'I think Bono without Ali would unleash an energy upon the world that might have as much negative effect as it has positive.'

*Adam Clayton, U2 by U2 (October 2006)*

'Mick [Jagger] is Mick, and must be avoided for one's own safety.'

*Andrea Corr, Q (July 1999)*

'Some of the most vicious hecklers tend to be women – especially drunk militant, separatist feminists. They are the most severe of hecklers!'

*Christy Moore, Hot Press (18 June 1987)*

'No one debates with [him]. It's not allowed. Every person that Van's got around him is a yes-person . . .'

*Singer Linda Gail Lewis, Can You Feel The Silence? A New Biography of Van Morrison by Clinton Heylin (Viking Books 2002)*

'The sensual warmth and dry wit of her way with a lyric makes you wonder why she isn't a bigger star and why any record company in their right mind would let her go.'

*Music writer David Hepworth on Mary Coughlan, Q (May 1994)*

'The people who know us can read between the lines. The people who listen to our records – they're not fooled by it. The fact of the matter is that we went to a lot of trouble to help Sinéad's career in the early days. And that's what you do, if you can ... Bono in particular pioneered Sinéad. He went to a lot of trouble encouraging her ... Edge used her on the soundtrack for *Captive*; there were various negotiations with Ensign Records [Sinéad O'Connor's first record label] that Ossie Kilkenny [then U2 accountant] was involved in – so she's talking crap ... It's stupid. It's immature. She'll learn. But I know damn well that she won't be making records in ten years. I was interested in her because I thought she was a great talent and I thought she had a future. That's why you support people. Now I'm not so sure that she has what it takes to last.'

*Adam Clayton on criticism from Sinéad O'Connor,* Hot Press *(October 1988)*

'Her voice conveys her personality – it's not just notes or a story, you get 100 per cent her. I love her stubbornness. It's not like she's twitching all the time, but when you see those eyes light up it's, "Fuckin' hell, here we go ..."'

*Massive Attack's Robert Del Naja on Sinéad O'Connor,* Mojo *(October 2005)*

# IRELAND/UPBRINGING/
# BEGINNINGS

A sense of Irishness is a singular thing; it's like being raised a Catholic: you can drift away, dissociate yourself from it, or even ignore it for years, but what was drummed into you from an early age remains with you for the rest of your life. The fact that identity is crucial to the formation of an individual is something that permeates Irish rock music; Cathal Coughlan's initial dismissal of his roots in the early days of Microdisney was eventually replaced by an embracing of them and afforded him the ability to create music that was imbued with such a sense of identity that it spoke with a Cork accent. Similarly, The Pogues: you'd never think that not all of them have Irish passports, such is the intrinsic nature of their music, which celebrates the woes and joys of the 'Paddy Experience' in a way that hasn't been touched on before or since. Ditto Van Morrison, Thin Lizzy, Boomtown Rats, U2, Divine Comedy and Sinéad O'Connor, each of whom have written about their Irishness and their upbringing in an eloquent and visceral fashion. It all boils down to this simple fact: you can take the Irish out of Ireland, but you can't take Ireland out of the Irish.

'Modena being the culinary capital of Italy and therefore, arguably, the world, Boyzone decide it is time to sample some delicious local fare. So they send out for McDonald's. "But this is Italy," protests the astonished production manager. "They're from Dublin," apologises [tour manager] Mark Plunkett.'

Q *(August 1999)*

'It was an open house, so there were hundreds of people coming in and out of it all the time, lots of gambling, drinking, music, dancing, singing and storytelling. All those things went together and made Ireland a better place to be than England.'

*Shane MacGowan,* Mojo *(September 2004)*

'I don't like Dublin. Never have. I detest it, to be honest. I think the people are snobs. I love Ireland, though. I love Cork, but I've never had a good time in Dublin.'

*The Fall's Mark E. Smith,* Hot Press *(30 November 1984)*

'Microdisney wasn't a collective but there was nonetheless a party line about a lot of things. Most of the guys weren't Irish and Sean's [O'Hagan, founding member of the band] link with the place was fairly tenuous, particularly emotionally. So I felt that if I put anything across through lyrics or interviews that was too identifiable with Ireland I was letting the side down. It was only in the last six months of Microdisney's life that I began to draw back and say, fair enough, I've been living in England for a while but I am Irish . . . Irish literature and music has had a strong effect on my consciousness and I still immerse myself in a lot of that. Some of my favourite singers, for example, are Irish. Christy Moore in particular is a big favourite of mine. The Stars of Heaven are another. So what the fuck was I doing submerging all of that and positively slagging it off?'

*Cathal Coughlan,* Hot Press *(14 June 1990)*

'The Divine Comedy, Brian Kennedy, Therapy? – there's one common link. They moved away from Northern Ireland, and to me that's the end of the debate. Nobody from here in the last 20 years has worked their way through the ranks on the local scene and gone on to large-scale success. It's sad, but it just can't be done.'

*Graphic designer/musician Rick Monro,* Mojo *(September 1997)*

'In 1976, no one went into Belfast city centre at night-time. It was the first time since the Troubles began that people started to go to Belfast venues like the Harp Bar and the Pound. The only people you saw in the street back then were either the army, the police or the punks. It was the first time in ten years that people started to get together – it didn't matter whether you were a Catholic or a Protestant. That is very much true – I'd spent ten years sitting at home, listening to records . . .'

*Terry Hooley,* D'Side *(April/May 1994)*

'The first time we rehearsed was in Johnnie Fingers' brother Pat's basement flat in Monkstown, outside Dublin. We did it for a laugh, as something for us to do in the afternoon, and it lasted no more than two hours because we were all cramped in this tiny room, it was roasting and the noise was intolerable. None of us knew what to do. Garry [Roberts] had this amp that winked blue, pink and yellow lights on and off in time with whatever you were playing. He plugged in his Telecaster and started doing the Doobie Brothers' "China Grove". I couldn't stand that sort of shit – I wanted to play Stealers Wheel songs – so immediately there was an argument, and that was pretty much normal for our career. Anyway, we were shite.'

*Bob Geldof,* Mojo *(May 2004)*

'I found a guitar in the house, a musician had left it there once and, eh, you know I was fascinated by it. As luck would have it when I was around nine I got an acoustic guitar and just started trying to teach myself. I couldn't even tune the guitar then . . . Luckily, across the road there was a man who used to play Hawaiian guitar and he tuned it for me. And then I'd a few of these little song books – Lonnie Donegan Skiffle Hits – and they have little chord symbols and diagrams to go with the songs, so I just put that together and started digging out the few chords and learning all the songs that Lonnie was doing . . . Most of the material Lonnie did was Woody Guthrie stuff or Leadbelly, so it was a good second-hand way of discovering these American songs. And then obviously at the time you had Fats Domino and Chuck Berry songs. You'd just learn everything you could within reason, and that's more or less how I started . . . It's almost like, teach yourself and, you know, discover for yourself, from the radio.'

*Rory Gallagher in conversation with Colm Keane, RTÉ Radio One (30 August 1985)*

'When I'm in Ireland I say I'm from Dublin; when I'm in Dublin I say I'm from Crumlin. When I'm in Crumlin I say I'm from Lakeland Road and when I'm in Lakeland Road I say I'm a Lynott.'

*Thin Lizzy's Phil Lynott, as quoted in* Mojo *(December 1993)*

'It's always an advantage being an outsider. Take [George Bernard] Shaw, for example, he was an Irishman living in London lampooning the English. My own songs have been an extension of that, exploring the outside view. I've always been amazed that bands like The Clash, for all their political awareness, have never successfully given a true perspective on their environment . . . The only band who got anywhere close were Squeeze with *East Side Story* as the English equivalent of what The Radiators were doing.'

*Radiators/Pogues member Philip Chevron,* Hot Press *(11 November 1983)*

# Rockaganda

'I see Ireland like a child that's been battered. We lost our history, we lost our language to the British. We have this emptiness because of what's been forgotten. The Irish people walk around feeling that ache all the time.'

*Sinéad O'Connor, Q (September 1994)*

'Four Dublin schoolboys carried off the top prize at the Limerick Civic Week Pop '78 Competition on Saturday night . . . U2 Malahide, the winning group, was made up of 16-year old Larry Mullen, of Rosemount Ave., Artane, an Intermediate Cert student at Mount Temple; Dave Evans (16), of St Margaret's Park, Malahide, who is doing his Leaving Cert; Adam Clayton (17), of Ard na Mara, Malahide, a Leaving Cert student, and Paul Hewson (17), of Cedarwood Rd, Ballymun, who is also doing his Leaving Cert. The group are just a year together and progressed from country music to "doing our own stuff". Paul Hewson said: "This means we can solve our money problems in a big way, particularly with regard to equipment. Now we hope to be able to buy a van." The boys had to promote themselves. "No one in Dublin was interested in us and we came down here as a last resort," said Adam Clayton, group leader. All the boys had praise for their school, which encouraged them and gave them facilities to practise. In particular, they appreciated the help of Mr Donald Moxham, History Teacher, and Mr Albert Bradshaw, Music Teacher, at the school. They appeared on RTÉ three weeks ago and they came to Limerick with the financial help of their parents – the trip cost them £60 – and the support of their fans who travelled with the group to see them triumph.'

*News report in the* Evening Press *(30 March 1978)*

'We rehearsed in The Pit, as we used to call my bedroom. We'd sometimes rehearse there for 30-date tours! We also practiced in a scout hut, because Feargal was a scout leader. Out first ever show was there a month after I joined. We did "Jumpin' Jack Flash" and "Back In The Night" by Dr Feelgood. Then we rehearsed in Mrs Simms' shed, as mentioned on the first album. She was Mickey's [Bradley] sister's mother-in-law. We sound-proofed it with bubble-wrap which Feargal got from working at Radio Rentals.'

*The Undertones' Damien O'Neill,* Mojo *(September 2000)*

'I like least the bitterness, the gossip. The thing I've noticed coming back here, is when you come home, they all say, "When are you goin' back?" It's the first question you get asked. It's not, "How long are you here for?" . . . I also dislike the hypocrisy . . . [Ireland] is begrudging to its own. But, by the same token, there is an awful lot who are very proud. I mean, I'm proud when I see U2 or the [Boomtown] Rats make it. However, I think it's an Irishman's right to knock Ireland, but I get offended if anybody foreign does it. There is the hypocrisy I'm talkin' about!'

*Phil Lynott,* Hot Press *(18 May 1984)*

'It is of cardinal importance that The Boomtown Rats were Irish. At the time you had Van Morrison doing his Yeats, mystic/Celtic thing, you had Phil Lynott, a black man from Crumlin, singing about Róisín Dubh and having a hit record with an old Irish folk tune, and you had a Corkman, Rory Gallagher, doing this US delta blues. But we were most definitely a Dublin suburban band. And punk was a very metropolitan thing; look at The Sex Pistols, The Clash, The Stranglers. We always got on best with The Pistols because Johnny Rotten was a Paddy – and we really saw ourselves as being part of the modern world. In fact, Bono once described us as being "the first of the moderns", which is essentially correct. But the way we felt about ourselves wasn't reflected in the country.'

*Bob Geldof,* The Irish Times *(October 2003)*

'The Clash in Belfast the first time? It was a fucking rescue mission even though they didn't play. The 'SS RUC' chant became a rallying cry. The kids were united. Back in the Europa Hotel [Joe, lead singer] Strummer was on the honey, his throat shattered. Mick [Jones, guitarist] was pontificating on the bed. It was my first question as a fanzine scribbler–cum–journo. "So what about the album?" The answer. "What about it?" Thanks Mick.'

*Gavin Martin, co-founder of Northern Ireland's best known punk fanzines,* Alternative Ulster, It Makes You Want To Spit *(Reekus Music 2003)*

# Ireland/Upbringing/Beginnings

'I believe everyone is sort of married to the place they're from. Summers are a magnet for all types, while in winter everything shuts down and it's only the solitary figures left, and time stretches and menace hangs over things.'

*Fionn Regan on his hometown of Bray, County Wicklow,* Mojo *(January 2007)*

'Ireland is so insular. You tend to think that everything revolves around you and where you are at the moment. For instance, I didn't realise how deep the sectarian thing was in Glasgow until we went there. I didn't realise they had 12th of July parades in Liverpool. Little things like that made me realize that Belfast wasn't completely isolated. I always thought it was.'

*Stiff Little Fingers member Jake Burns,* Hot Press *(11 February 1988)*

'I can remember in the Sixties, to be from Ireland was a disadvantage . . . you were fucked . . . We were ostracized. Even if you were a rock star! You were just Paddy.'

*Van Morrison,* Q *(August 1993)*

'We've never pushed that [Irish] aspect of the band. With a band like the [Hothouse] Flowers it's obvious that they're Irish, you can see it and hear it, but I absolutely refuse to depend on the Irish ex-pats anywhere in the world. It's fine when they come along to the gigs, I'm glad to see them and for them it's probably a little bit of home for the night and they can get off on that, that's cool. But to go, for instance, and sell out the Mean Fiddler has to be taken with pinch of salt because you're playing to the same people you'd be playing to if you were in the Stadium, the Baggot or whatever.'

*Something Happens drummer Eamonn Ryan,* Hot Press *(28 June 1990)*

'It would be a logical extension for us, really, to use the primary instruments of our line-up and ally it to dance rhythms. But we would have to preserve the songs. I don't know whether it's because I'm from Cavan, but I just can't sit down and write a song about checking out the groove. I think I'd get hit across the head by my mother!'

*Barry Walshe of The Fireflys,* In Dublin *(23 May 1991)*

'I loved every minute of it. We were scamming it, chancing our arm. Then it became real: the music began to sound right, the interviews began to sound like real interviews and the clothes we were wearing became real clothes.'

*Ronan Keating,* Q *(September 2000)*

'People say that they're drunken yobbos from Finglas and Ballymun. That's nonsense. They're kind, caring blokes but they're just like a bunch of children. They need a father figure, someone to tell them to cop themselves on. I remember fights breaking out over cans of coke and things like that. Sometimes the lads' balls would be bigger than their brains. If you had a word with them they'd listen to you. But, Jesus, you had to keep an eye on them.'

*Aslan's first manager, Dick Fagan, on his young charges,* Hot Press *(20 October 1988)*

'My Irishness was never something I hid or camouflaged. I grew up in a strong Irish community. Of course, early on I'd be teased about it, I was called "Paddy" from an early age. I mean, there I was, born, braised and bred in Manchester but I was still always called "Paddy". And this was back in the 1960s when it was a bitter and malevolent slur. But that's how Manchester people are – they're extremely critical of everything and everybody.'

*Morrissey,* The Irish Times *(November 1999)*

'There was an incident at school which the staff will remember. A science teacher called "Thompy" Steele had a few words with Van [Morrison]. His whole life was revolving around music and Thompy said, Van, you'd do better to concentrate on your school work because you'll never make a living at this music lark.'

*Walter Blakely, neighbour of Van Morrison's,* Mojo *(November 1993)*

'Maybe it's just getting older and the whole blah blah that goes with that, but I would like to go back to Cork more often than I have done in recent years. I think a large part of the disdain with which I viewed the place stemmed from a feeling of pique on my part. It's a very difficult place to go back to unless you've got some great achievements to report, so I always found it difficult to go back there, especially in the last few years – I'm not the kind of person who likes bragging about their troubles. But fuck it, my attitude now is that provided I'm allowed regulate my own environment, I could probably manage to live there for a couple of weeks before getting hot under the collar, and let's face it, that's as much as you can say in defence of any locale.'

*Cathal Coughlan,* Hot Press *(14 June 1990)*

'Two fellows from Cork lived near us. One was named Frank, the other Walter. They used to do unusual things like directing traffic out in the street or dressing up in bus conductors' uniforms and collecting bus fares. They used to have a certain unusual way of walking and running, and if we saw anyone who did something equally daft or had similar characteristics, we'd say that they were a bit of a Frank and Walter. Then the band name came.'

*Paul Linehan of you-know-who,* Hot Press *(23 April 1992)*

'Eventually, it would just eat you up, and you'd just decide you're getting claustrophobia there and you had to do or die and . . . start a band properly.'

*Rory Gallagher on playing in showbands. In conversation with Colm Keane, RTÉ Radio One (30 August 1985)*

## Ireland/Upbringing/Beginnings

'The way I see it, there's only two choices for people here [Ireland]: either to go mad or kill yourself.'

*Sinéad O'Connor, Q (September 1994)*

'We were told we were going to be the Irish answer to Take That, and I wanted all of that. I wanted to have number one albums, tour the world with music and songs. I wanted to hear our songs on the radio. Before we knew it, we were there and that was quite scary, because we always thought there was someone better than us. That was one of the good things about Boyzone – we never really believed the hype about us too much, or that we were real superstars. As a band we always had our feet on the ground, and I think it was the Irishness in us that generated that.'

*Ronan Keating,* Cara Magazine *(March 2001)*

'It's one thing the Irish have. Give Sinéad [O'Connor] a kick and she'd stay there and scream about it. Kick Bono and he'd kiss you. Give Liam [Ó Maonlaí] a kick and he'd probably start jamming with you. There's a pig-headed Celtic belief in yourself. That's why Irish bands go down well in America: oh, man, they're *real*. But kick some English bands . . . they'd start crying.'

*Gavin Friday, Q (April 1992)*

'People in Dublin could never grasp the fact that before Horslips there was nothing for the rest of Ireland. Okay, there was Rory Gallagher and Thin Lizzy, but they'd be the one-trip-a-year-to-the-National-Stadium thing. The Lipsos used to come around the country – the only show in town, and effectively the only reason to remain alive'

*Declan Lynch,* In Dublin *(2 January 1997)*

'It was hard to get gigs, especially when the hair grew long and we gained a reputation for having a nonchalant attitude. All the other local groups wore identical suits and we just weren't like that. We were five individuals and we wore what we fancied wearing. Van had brilliant phrasing for the blues. He never did have a personality but he got carried away at times. We would have great fun together and then he would change. He was a very changeable character. Very definitely a nonconformist.'

*Billy Harrison, founding member of Them,* Mojo *(November 1993)*

'U2's early Irish struggles were their Hamburg that steeled them ... All their later hurdles shrank in comparison with that of an Irish band jumping the Beecher's Brook to a recording deal, ten years ago. Yet that alone wouldn't have sustained their momentum down all the days of the decade. For other Irish acts, distance has often meant isolation from useful influences, but U2 got the balance right. Instead, distance inoculated them from the false lures of fashion and reinforced their sense of crusade. For U2 were unusual because they dared to hope in a decade of mean-spiritedness and political illusionists like Ronald Reagan ... I'd insist their hopefulness was Irish. Working in rock, a new form for the Irish, U2 escaped being burdened by history. They weren't authors, oppressed by the shadows of Yeats, Joyce, Beckett or Anthony Cronin's lost Fifties generation of McDaid's. But neither were they an English band, handicapped by that culture's confusion of values and increasing spiritual resentment at its self-consciousness.'

*Bill Graham,* Hot Press *(December 1989)*

'So sad, so small, so insular. There's a lot of grudges in Ireland. There's a famous story Bono once told: American guy driving around sees this mansion on the hill. Someday, he says, I'll have that house. Irish guy sees the same mansion. Someday, he says, I'll get that bastard. That's the Irish attitude.'

*Ronan Keating,* Q *(September 2000)*

'I used to come back to Dublin a lot when I was younger. We'd go back to Crumlin and of course I saw it with a child's vision, but the people seemed happier and more carefree and Crumlin seemed so open – certainly more so than the confines of Hulme. We were quite happy to ghettoise ourselves as the Irish community in Manchester, the Irish stuck rigidly together and there'd always be a relation living two doors down, around the back or up the passage. It always struck me as quite odd that people who had lived twenty or thirty years in Manchester still spoke with the broadest and the sharpest Pearse Street accent. [Emigrant Irish culture] seeped into everything I knew growing up. I was very aware of being Irish and we were told that we were quite separate from the scruffy kids

around us – we were different to them . . . It was always odd
later on with The Smiths when I was described as being
"extremely English" because other people would tell me
that I looked Irish, I sounded Irish and had other telltale
signs . . . It's funny, because U2 are always portrayed as being
famously Irish and this is the great unsaid: aren't half the
band English? All you have to do is hear The Smiths'
surnames - Maher, Morrissey, Joyce and Rourke. It was
only actually Andy Rourke's mother who was an English
parent - all the other parents were Irish.'

*Morrissey,* The Irish Times *(November 1999)*

'I really think the Irish are the European Jews. They've
got a greater diaspora, almost. Without question, their
contribution to twentieth century intellectual life is
enormous. I mean the idea that the Irish leave, is
embodied in us. The other thing was that I was raised
Catholic and you never rid yourself of the voodoo. And
the Irish look out, they're not insular, they must do.'

*Bob Geldof,* Hot Press *(6 September 1990)*

'(Dublin) was a shithole . . . It's a really bad music scene –
we didn't see any point in staying there anymore. We went
to Holland because we wanted to go anywhere but
London. It's such a cliche - you know, "going to London."
Just about every Irish band that went to London never
made it. Just think of it, every Irish band that went to
London, where are they now? . . . Irish bands – they don't
do anything. They are so obsessed with major record

companies and getting deals and cracking America and all this garbage that in the end, they're like nowhere . . . They're running around trying to do everything, trying to be rock stars but in the end they aren't achieving. That's . . . why we got out of Dublin, because Dublin is so stifling . . . When we were there, there were a lot of people quite happy with their situation. A lot of bands who felt snug – or maybe smug – with their situation . . . Every band who thinks it's got the stadium potential. Of U2 – Cactus World News, Blue In Heaven – why did they think they could make it? They have to do something of their own . . . But all those other bands – they are all like just little U2s. That's not saying that their music is the same, but they have to understand that they've all been signed on the strength of what happened in Ireland with U2, basically, not on the strength of what they're doing . . . But I just really hate the Irish music scene . . . I've lived in Holland, Berlin and London – I know what music scenes are like and I know that it's unnecessarily shit. There's a real stupid attitude there.'

*My Bloody Valentine's Kevin Shields,* Hot Press *(24 August 1989)*


'She used to keep this bag of peanuts in the kitchen and maybe someone took a handful. So I'd be lined up with my two brothers and my sister, my mother with the Bible in one hand and a hockey stick in the other to beat the shit out of us. She liked to humiliate us; she liked us to beg her for mercy. And these sessions would go on for hours. It was extremely violent, but the abuse was sexual too. It need not always be about touching. Though that's not to say she didn't touch us. One thing she did regularly was make me take all my clothes off and force me to lie on the floor and she would stamp on my abdomen with the intention of bursting my womb. That's what she said, I'm going to burst you.'

*Sinéad O'Connor, Q (September 1994)*

'I knew I was gonna do music, way back, way back. There was never any doubt. When I was three, I knew.'

*Van Morrison, quoted in* Can You Feel The Silence? A New Biography of Van Morrison *by Clinton Heylin (Viking Books 2002)*

'It was so hard for years. I remember we used to travel in a mini-van with the garden chair in the back.' (Sharon). 'The garden chair was the comfortable one. I tucked my bottom between the two seats.' (Andrea). 'We rehearsed and rehearsed and rehearsed in front of mirrors in a dusty old house. It was Jim's. He never cleaned it.' (Sharon).

*The Corr sisters recall the good old days, Q (February 1999)*

'Saturday night was special – if you weren't taking your date to the pictures, you could go down to Bangor to the Duckpond or Cloud Nine. If you wanted to stay in Belfast you had a choice of places to go depending on who was playing. The Plaza was out . . . and so were the Fiesta Ballroom, the Embassy Club, the Boom Boom Rooms and many others. The reason being that if you didn't look like one of The Munsters or have thirty mates with you all six foot five, you might not live too long. So we went to places like Clarkes, The Astor, Betty Staffs, The Elizabethan, C.I.M.S., The Belmont Tennis Club, to name a few, and only to places like Romanoes when the Radio One Club was being broadcast from there. In those days there were no shortage of places to go; now there are none. At this point I would like to throw in the names of a few Belfast bands I used to go and see. Bands like Sam Mahood and the Big Soul Foundation, The Alleykatz, The Setz, Just Five, Creative Mind, The Mad Lads, The People, Aztecs, The Few, Luigi Crum and the Comebacks, The Fugitives, not to mention Them, Sunshine, Spectres, Five By Five, Beeswax, The Blue Angels, Mystics and hundreds more. But before you went to see any of the groups on a Saturday, at tea-time you watched Juke Box Jury or Thank Your Lucky Stars. Even your habits had to change on a Friday night with the introduction of Ready Steady Go.'

*Good Vibrations supremo Terri Hooley recalls Belfast in the 1960s,* Hot Press *(4 September 1981)*

'I've always felt pulled to Ireland because my mother was Irish but whenever I've gone, I've never felt very at home.'
*Kate Bush,* Q *(October 1993)*

'I've been doing English radio interviews all week and they seem to think that everybody in Ireland plays the fiddle! My accent and phrasing couldn't come from anywhere else but Cork, but I'm only now discovering what it is to be Irish as I travel abroad.'

*Sinéad Lohan, Q (July 1996)*

'Absolutely. I wouldn't spout this Anglophile drivel otherwise, would I?'

*Divine Comedy's Neil Hannon on whether his Irishness has any bearing on his work, Q (May 1994)*

'I go back to Ireland to the extent I don't feel I've left it. Emotionally, I don't regard myself as in exile, because I tour so much – I pop back to Ireland so I don't feel like James Joyce.'

*Rory Gallagher in conversation with Colm Keane, RTÉ Radio One (30 August 1985)*

'We got a reputation in Dundalk because there was three of us behind the bar. The students would be there ogling.'

*Sharon Corr, Q (February 1999)*

'In Ireland [Skid Row] were underrated, but everybody was underrated in Ireland – and they probably still are. The way it is – or when I was here – was that people weren't encouraged to do anything original. It was always like, "yeah, you can play if you do cover versions of Top 40 material." But there was never any incentive to do anything for yourself . . . When I joined the band we were doin' all kinds of weird stuff. It was one of the things that attracted me to them. Phil [Lynott] was just singin' then and getting weird sounds with echo machines. We were doin' a lot of American-style stuff, which I quite liked. Did we make any money out of it? No, not really.'

*Gary Moore,* Hot Press *(15 February 1985*

'My family were real '70s people. They had big parties. Crazy parties. My dad would barbecue naked apart from an apron. He had the big hairy chest, the medallion, the whole thing. We had a big house, had some money. He made bar furniture, which gave him an excuse to spend most of his time in the pub. (My mother) . . . Gorgeous legs up to there, a trophy bride for my dad. Part of me is trying to be her, and a part of me is totally horrified by the idea.'

*Róisín Murphy,* Q *(September 2000)*

'I think of myself as an Irishman first, black second.'

*Phil Lynott, as quoted in* Mojo *(December 1993)*

'I had tried to get a group together at school, which lasted one night! I was still doing the odd show on my own – talent shows and charity shows, pioneer rallies. So when I saw an ad in a paper – "Showband needs guitar player" – I said, Well, I'll give it a bash. These fellas were doing two or three gigs a week and I could plug into an AC30 – the amplifier I had at home was a four-watt Selmer! I handled the rock 'n' roll department, basically. The two years I had with them was fun – at the age of 16 I was playing the showband gigs in England in Lent – which gave me the chance on nights off to go down to the Marquee and see The Yardbirds or Spencer Davis.'

*Rory Gallagher, as quoted in* Mojo *(October 1998)*

# LOVE AND FRIENDSHIP

O f all the topics that infiltrate the lyrical content of songs it is surely love and all its manifestations (the celebration of, the misery of, the emotional fallout, the doubt, the confusion, the wonder, et al) that feature throughout. It is rare that love and/or friendship runs smoothly, rare that feet can be kept on the ground when fans gather backstage to throw praise or to offer other items of their appreciation. The finest lyricists are those that are able to distil the best and the worst of love going right and love gone wrong into a four-minute song: Snow Patrol's Gary Lightbody is able to do this, seemingly effortlessly; as is Divine Comedy's Neil Hannon, Dave Couse (formerly of A House) and U2's Bono. But it's not just about the music. Real, genuine love — which sometimes involves real, genuine sex — occurs between band mates. It doesn't always last, but at least the participants know some great songs will be born out of their mutual despair. Cynical? Don't think for a second that the lovers don't think about this at least once a day.

❖

'I should be shot for the things I've done to women. I've always been the bastard. I've always spoiled the happy ending.'

*Gary Lightbody (Snow Patrol), Q (August 2004)*


'I was sorry to see it go . . . Everybody thought it was a scam, that we'd be back together again in six months. Maybe it's because I'm such a proficient liar . . . but there was no way around it, it was definitely goin' to end. And now it's gone, it's never goin' to come back. It's like your virginity . . . that's the way I feel. It was a good band, I was very pleased to be in it.'

*Phil Lynott on the break-up of Thin Lizzy, Hot Press (18 May 1984)*


'There have been times in my marriage when I thought about those . . . nights out, those great girls that showed such promise. Now, with a little experience I think I know what that night would have looked like . . . But it's not easy to deal with money, it's not easy to deal with fame, it's not easy to deal with women throwing themselves at you, even being married, perhaps especially being married. No matter how strong you are, no matter how upright, these are real hurdles that you have to figure out how to get over. I will never forget the time Adam saw me in a headlock with some starlet and said to me, "It's fun. It's exciting having sex with someone you don't know . . . It's a great adventure getting to know somebody. But as rare as it is to fall in love, it is not as rare as real love, I will die for you love, I will be there when you're sick and when you're frail love. Now that's rare. I would give everything, all these experiences that I'm having, all these different and extraordinary women, I'd give them all up for what you have." I remember Adam telling me that. And if there was one reason for having him as best man at my wedding, that was it, that one conversation.'

*Bono,* U2 by U2 *(October 2006)*

'"It was before Backwards Into Paradise, wasn't it?" queries Rachel [Tighe] as the exact date of the beginning of their relationship is pondered. "It was on my twenty-first birthday," Dave [Long] recollects. "I was at a party in the Harp Bar. I had it there because Echo and the Bunnymen's 'Killing Moon' was on the jukebox. I played it all the time. Rachel turned up for some strange reason. She wasn't invited – she was with my brother. I went, 'oh, I like her'. Then about six months later we met up in the local pub and started going out together."

"You called me a witch."

"Yeah, I called her a witch because she used to have black hair just like Gerry Whelan's of An Emotional Fish. Remember all the jokes about your hair and make-up? She was kind of striking actually . . ."

When they split up was there ever a problem of jealousy when either of them brought their respective new partners into the band environment? There is a pause longer than the gestation period for an elephant. Says Rachel, understatement mixed with nervous laughter, "There were a couple of dodgy situations, alright."

"Yes, there was," concurs Dave, "but I don't think they're for printing . . . let's put it this way, I wasn't for certain situations, virtually to the stage of saying, are you sure you want to do this? It would have been like if one of the other band members had started going out with Rachel six months after we split up. Now that would have freaked me out. I would have had serious problems with that, which is a terrible thing to say I know. There's none of the New Man ethic there, do you know what I mean? But now I could live with it.'"

*Into Paradise's Dave Long and Rachel Tighe on falling in and out of love while in a rock band,* Hot Press *(18 October 1992)*

'Three . . . but that's only mid-week. Weekends we're not married at all. It's a special dispensation we got off the Pope.'

*Aslan's Christy Dignam on being asked how many of the band are married,* D'Side *(August/September 1994)*

'We basically graduated April 2007, when we went to America. I guess it would be a lie to say there wasn't some kind of . . . John kept on saying to us, "I'm watching the dailies, and there's definitely something" – 'cos he wouldn't let us watch them. He said, "I guarantee you two, at some point, will have a relationship." And I said, "Dude, fuck off!" Even though I guess I probably knew the same, but he kept jokingly calling us his Bogart and Bacall . . . And he was right. It took a little longer than he thought. And I think he, what's the word, not exploited, but used whatever tension there was. Like you say, there wasn't a lot of acting.'

*The Frames' member and Oscar winner Glen Hansard on his then burgeoning relationship with* Once *co-star Marketa Irglova,* Hot Press *(26 March 2008)*

'There's a certain serendipity about Bob seeing that news report [BBC's Michael Buerk's report on famine in Africa], because it came at a time when he could really follow through with the idea. And a tragedy on that scale needs a Bob Geldof, because no one has that sort of drive. He's Forrest Gump. Hand him a ball and he'll run forever.'

*Johnny Fingers,* Mojo *(May 2005)*

'I know a lot of homosexual men and most of them I get on with. Some overtly camp men I don't get on with. But it all comes down to love. How can anyone attack love? I could never attack love.'

*Bono,* Hot Press *(March 1987)*

'I wasn't able and I'm not able and I don't think I'll ever be able to conduct a relationship on an intimate level with another human being in terms of a lover.'

*Sinéad O'Connor,* Q *(September 1994)*

'Something strange happened towards the end of *The Joshua Tree* tour. We had campaigned for Martin Luther King Day in Tempe, Arizona, where the tour opened . . . We went back to Tempe at the end of the tour . . . I was getting death threats throughout the tour. One in particular was taken very seriously by the FBI. This character was a racist offended by our work, he thought we were messing in other people's business and taking sides with the black man. One night the FBI said, "Look, it's quite serious. He says he has a ticket. He said he's armed. And he said if you sing "Pride (In The Name Of Love)", he's going to shoot you. So we played the show, the FBI were around, everyone was a little unnerved. You just didn't know – could be in the building? Up in the rafters? On the roof? During "Pride" . . . I was singing the third verse, "Early morning April 4, a shot rings out in a Memphis sky." I just closed my eyes and sang. And when I opened my eyes, Adam was standing in front of me.'

*Bono*, U2 by U2 *(October 2006)*

'The first time I met Luke Kelly . . . [he] was enthralling a bunch of Joyce-hunting Americans who were entertaining him like a real Irish king. A train of gin and tonics were placed on the table before him as he declaimed poetry and song in a rich and vaguely nasal Dub shout that filled the whole pub, blow-dried the blue rinses and filled their oh-my-gaads with kulcher . . . The second time I met Luke was at a gig we both played in the North Star Hotel . . . Red beret rammed down on his enormous red head, [a] voice as rich as bejasus bellowing out the rallying cry. Spine-chilling stuff . . . But what struck me most that night was the head, the incredible medusa-tangle-ginger-curls massiveness of it, and the amazing rocks, wrinkles, crevices, canyons that were sculpted, no, hewn into it. Jesus Christ, said one of my companions, there's a face that's been really lived in . . . The last time I met Luke was in The Viking in Dame Street . . . Into this maelstrom walked Luke and Madeleine. Well, it was after the first tumour. And there was something tragic about it – he was the same man all right, but a bit slower and a lot more subdued. And with the bottle of soda water, the pathos was complete. My heart was broken . . . And who was at his funeral, remembered by his own? Just Joe and Mary Soap for the most part, although Charlie Haughey made it too. Apart from the thousands of ordinary people, and musicians, it seemed right to have the Workers Party, the Communist Party and Michael D [Higgins] on hand. And nobody from Fine Gael. Luke would have seen the rightness of that . . . "He had no time for religion," said Fr Michael Cleary, "but he had great faith." My arse. What Luke had was a great voice. And soul.'

*Excerpts from an obituary of The Dubliners' Luke Kelly, Dermot Stokes,* Hot Press *(10 February 1984)*

'That relationship was based on trust and honesty, and I changed away from that . . . I wasn't honest. I feel like I cheated, I broke my word. I put an awful lot of unhappiness into her life . . . I feel that people, in general, put an awful lot of misery into each other's lives and can progress too easily from loving someone so much that they end up suffocating each other . . . I found myself in situations that I'd always dreamed about. I've always been one of those people who wanted to experience life and see what it was all about, because I don't think you can really write unless you've done that. You can't write from the confines of a one-bedroomed flat, living with the same person every day in a very safe environment. Most teenagers, and I was certainly one of them, would read about rock bands and have this fantastic impression of what they were doing and what they were up to, living life to the full and often paying the full price for it. I knew it was being offered to me, albeit on a smaller level, but I wanted to know what a bit of that was like, and that became impossible to do and keep a relationship together.'

*Something Happens frontman, Tom Dunne,* Hot Press *(28 June 1990)*

'It means a completely different thing to women than it does to men . . . But you've got to be very careful with what you are doing. You just don't give it away . . . Make sure they know what they have in their presence. It's far too precious to give to any old fucker.'

*Sinéad O'Connor on love,* Hot Press *(12 December 1991)*

# WHAT OTHERS SAY ABOUT US

People talk. People gossip. People state nice things. People utter nasty things. People tell the truth. People tell lies. What more can we say?

'Phillip thought he was bulletproof.'
*Thin Lizzy road manager Frank Murray, on the band's frontman, Phil Lynott,* Mojo *(December 1993)*

'What to make of this band who sound like The Osmonds, think like Richard Branson and drink like Thin Lizzy?'
*Adrian Deevoy on Boyzone,* Q *(August 1999)*

'Hats off to all the Pogues – for music the colour of tobacco smoke and alcohol, sad dreams, underdogs and lost love.'
*Film director Jim Jarmusch, the sleeve notes to the re-issued album,* Red Roses For Me *(Warner Strategic Marketing 2004)*

'He had that romantic idea of the rock 'n' roller, living outside the law. And Phil was a magnet. He loved having people around. You'd go over to his house and there'd be people there all the time! That's why his wife couldn't take it any longer. I almost think he had a fear of being alone.'

*Thin Lizzy guitarist Scott Gorham on band frontman Phil Lynott,* Mojo *(February 2006)*

'I love what [U2] have done. It's fucking great that an Irish band can leave such a mark on the world.'

*Bob Geldof,* Hot Press *(December 1989)*

'One of the Top Ten guitar players of all time but more importantly one of the Top Ten good guys.'

*Bono on Rory Gallagher, as quoted in* Mojo *(October 1998)*

'I'll walk into the pub and some old guy will go, "Larry, yer man Bono, he's a fucking eejit".'

*Larry Mullen Jr on being accosted by strangers in Dublin,* Q *(November 2004)*

'The cleaning ladies at Windmill Studios are teasing the Virgin Prunes. "U2 always wash up after themselves, they're clean. You leave things like hair all over the place. U2 are nice boys. You might be nice but they're clean."'

Hot Press *(13 May 1983)*

'The Frank and Walters look a bit of a mess, but there's nothing that a half-decent makeover and a visit to the dentist wouldn't put right.'

*John Aizlewood on Cork's curious moptops,* Q *(December 1992)*

## What Others Say About Us

'"He's a genius!" enthuses a soldier on the train ... "Magic!" says the cab driver, who doesn't buy records any more but listens to what his niece brings round. "Oh, he's so big-headed," says Shelley, a lean, lively blonde girl who sings with a Newcastle punk band called Screaming Targets.'

*Opinions on Bob Geldof,* NME *(20 October 1979)*

'Bono makes us all proud to be human.'

*Tom Cruise, as quoted in* Q *(August 2004)*

'Bono's a churchman of sorts and he understands the power of singing on top of your range. It's an exorcism.'

*Regular U2 record producer Daniel Lanois,* Mojo *(January 2008)*

'His sort of character just doesn't exist in the music business. In fact, it doesn't exist in any industry. He was just a wonderful human being.'

*Rory Gallagher's colleague Mark Feltham,* Mojo *(October 1998)*

'I admire him very much not only for his very fierce intelligence and a powerful articulacy, which would put most politicians to shame, but for the fact that he's somebody who's been given a moment of money, influence, fame and he used it to parlay it into something else, and to stay that way. He's also a quintessentially new Irishman in that he's a phenomenally successful businessman.'

*Roy Foster on Bob Geldof,* Luck and the Irish – a Brief History of Change, 1970–2000 *(Published by Allen Lane 2007)*

'They're like the Dead End Kids on a leaky boat.'
*Tom Waits on The Pogues,* Mojo *(September 2004)*

'She got a typical New York welcome. The audience put her to the test and she just wasn't up to it. Don't ask me to feel any sympathy for her.'
*Neil Young on the negative reaction to Sinéad O'Connor's appearance at Bob Dylan's thirtieth anniversary concert at Madison Square Garden in October 1992,* Q *(January 1993)*

'There wasn't anyone in that period of Irish music for younger folk to revere, apart from the likes of Dickie Rock or Brendan Bowyer. Rory [Gallagher] was the first to get out there and do it properly. He became a hero to a whole load of people who didn't know anything about the blues.'
*Henry McCullough,* Mojo *(October 1998)*

'The stadium-rock-meets-Protestant-evangelical note of their music is something I'm more than iffy about. Again, he's somebody who has used great wealth and fame to essentially pursue worthwhile ends, and I'm not, as my son would say, going to diss him for that.'
*Roy Foster on Bono,* Luck and the Irish – a Brief History of Change, 1970–2000. *(Published by Allen Lane 2007)*

'I believe I look like Bono – there ain't nothing wrong in looking like Bono.'
*Actor Tom Hanks on his character in* The Da Vinci Code, *Jonathan Ross Show (11 January 2008)*

# What Others Say About Us

'Built like a sex-powered high jumper, with the ability to write songs that inwardly laughed while they offered you 'outside' [for a fight] or promised to shag you senseless, [Phil] Lynott was the first self-constructed, self-conscious Irish rock star – deified in Dublin and Belfast alike, idolized by U2, Ash, Therapy? and Bob Geldof.'

Q *(March 1996)*

'Thin Lizzy's songs are timeless. They're almost all about drinking and fighting. That's what you really want from a rock band.'

*Smashing Pumpkins' kingpin, Billy Corgan,* Mojo *(February 2006)*

*Former* NME *writer Nick Kent on the following:*

U2: 'They redeemed themselves with their last two albums, but I really disliked them in the early days. I had a thing against them, but give them their due. It'll be really interesting to see what they come up with next . . . I still feel they're not talented enough to take on being The Best Group In The World, even if their sales figures, image and general demeanour lends itself to that title.'

*Van Morrison:* 'I have great respect for him. He is maybe the greatest white soul singer alive, and possibly the greatest soul singer alive, period. Truly extraordinary. I feel that the spiritual odyssey he was on ran down somewhere around 1978 and *Into The Music.* That was his last astonishing album. Then he got bogged down in a kind of . . . I don't want to say quasi-mystical, but it just didn't ring true with me . . . You know, whenever I hear Georgie Fame, I think of Hush Puppies. You know what I'm saying?'

*Bob Geldof*: 'He and I were like me and John Lydon — enemies from the very beginning for reasons that I don't really want to put into print. The music he makes is fundamentally talentless, but I have a lot of respect for him as a force and what he did for Live Aid. The man's charisma and intelligence are undeniable.'

*Phil Lynott*: 'I really liked him. I knew him quite well . . . A good guy. I really thought he'd live. He was one of the strongest ones, he seemed like a lion to me sometimes . . . He always looked so well, but I didn't see him for the last several years of his life, so obviously things got very bad for him. But I loved Thin Lizzy's early stuff - the mid-Seventies. One of the best bands of that time. Fabulous. Drugs took something from him, though. It took the talent from him and turned him into a cartoon.'

*Chris de Burgh*: 'Who's he? Oh yeah, "Lady In Red" . . . God I despise the man. Just despise him. I remember when I was coming off drugs he had a record out, and I had no record player, 'cos I was living with my parents in their retirement cottage in Swindon. I was living in a spare room and there was a radio there. So I listened to the radio most of the time, and De Burgh's "Lady In Red" was played over and over again. I hated it. And then I saw him on television and I hated him even more. The feeling I get off him is that he's so insincere. Truly insincere...'

Hot Press *(10 August 1994)*

'He fancied himself as an outlaw and a renegade, and he used those images in his songs. I used to ask him what it was like being young and black and living in Crumlin and he said, It's no worse than having cauliflower ears: you stick out but nobody says anything.'

*Irish artist Jim Fitzpatrick on Phil Lynott,* Mojo *(December 1993)*

'Spending time with Bono is like eating dinner on a train. Feels like you're moving, going somewhere.'

*Bob Dylan,* Chronicles Volume One *(Simon & Schuster 2004)*

'Rory [Gallagher] did have a strange personality. People would see the band onstage and imagine Rory was some sort of real wild guy. But he wasn't like that. For the two hours we gigged he was Rory; for the other 22 hours of the day he was some other bloke. Didn't have a lot of close friends. Did his own thing. Didn't really mix with other people bar saying hello and shaking hands. In fact, during our whole period together there was never any association with women. It sounds stupid, but he was just a really nice guy and very, very shy.'

*Taste's John Wilson,* Mojo *(October 1998)*

'Shane's lyrics bring me to a place that I know. I know his country, I've been through his meadow, across his bog, down his street and I love his work dearly. He is a man of words and raw emotion and understated pain that comes crawling out of the lyrics like the madness crawling out of the mountains.'

*Christy Moore on The Pogues,* Mojo *(September 2004)*

### The Van Morrison Corner

'When he's on a bad day he's just beyond awful, that's how he is.'

*Music promoter Harvey Goldsmith,* Can You Feel The Silence? A New Biography of Van Morrison *by Clinton Heylin (Viking Books 2002)*

'On stage there's no one to touch him; off stage he's unbearable.'

*Harvey Goldsmith (again), as quoted in* Mojo *(February 2008)*

'The man was a pig.'

*[And while we're at it], Spike Milligan on Van Morrison, as quoted in* Mojo *(February 2008)*

'As an artist he's clearly a genius. As a man he's impossible. He used to drop into the record company office, usually to harangue someone about some imagined slight, and people would literally hide in the cupboards so as not to have to confront him. It was never a case of,

## What Others Say About Us

"Wow, it's Van Morrison." People were actually terrified of him.'

*Anonymous press officer who used to work with Van Morrison in the 1980s,* Uncut *(July 2005)*

# LORD, IT'S HARD TO BE HUMBLE

For all the ego-tripping going on in rock music there are moments of reflection wherein even the most self-fancying of people take time out (hopefully not in front of a mirror) from their busy lives and come to the realisation that this success/fame/wealth lark isn't all it's cracked up to be. These ruminative periods of time, however, are well and truly shattered when a spotlight shines on them. In other words, grab humility when it's presented to you – it might take ages for it to be volunteered again.

'You get used to people runnin' around after you, carryin' your guitar case, doin' this, that and the other. When it's done constantly you start to take it for granted. You start expecting the amps to be ready when you walk into play, the equipment to be set up. Obviously, I'll still expect that in certain situations. For rehearsals I don't mind settin' everythin' up. I do mind if I'm paying somebody to do it, like in the Lizzy situation. Because people treat you as important, you begin to think that maybe you're a little bit more important than you are. You always have to look in the mirror, though.'

*Phil Lynott,* Hot Press *(18 May 1984)*


'I'm all for it. Like, why wait until I'm dead? Why not get all that stuff that happens to dead people now? I could come up with a deal. Maybe we could let the tourist buses in.'

Bono on Bono *[on being asked has his birthday become a public holiday in Ireland] (2005)*


'We know we have it very easy. That's just the game we're in. We're not claiming to be a super-talented rock band who write all our own music. We're singers.'

*Westlife's Shane Filan,* Q *(July 2000)*


'Bono's greatest talent is that he has a nose for a room and an instinct on how to work it. He's so brimming with talent that it's unbelievable.'

*Michael Colgan, director of Dublin's Gate Theatre,* Irish Independent *(31 March 2006)*


'We never had illusions that we could make a difference – although there may have been once or twice where we helped changed perceptions, but only in the right people.'

*Philip Chevron on the importance of The Radiators (from Space),* The Irish Times *(June 2004)*

# Rockaganda

'It's all very well after the first album to go around acting like stars in Ireland and fool yourself, but that's bullshit. We realized months ago that we couldn't keep up that attitude which you tend to have after coming back from a really good tour of America and everything's really good and you start to think, Christ, we're really on top of the world now! It dawns on you a month later that you're really no one, that you haven't sold many records and that if you don't do something the next time around, you're going to be in fucking big trouble.'

*Dave Couse (formerly of A House),* Hot Press *(December 1989)*

'I'd feel guilty if I started to complain . . . When I'm around people for a long time I start to get edgy. I'm not into the party scene. If anything, I just like to wait until I get home and a have a good night out with my friends. I'm not into any pretentious stuff. Showbiz parties? I feel as if I'm being watched all the time. So I have evenings off, and I love to relax, just to get into my pyjamas, jump into bed, watch TV, and order room service. Not very showbiz at all, is it?'

*Samantha Mumba,* The World of Hibernia *(Autumn 2001)*

'I never complain about what I do. I write every day, I go to gigs, I read – there really is little more to my life than that. I walk around Regent's Park and say hello to Paul McCartney.'

*Marc Carroll,* The Irish Times *(November 2005)*

# WHERE ARE THEY NOW?/VOICES FROM THE PAST

Ah, the promo T-shirt syndrome once again raises its head. The music industry is peculiar in that it will always be populated by bands/acts that aspire to simply getting signed. Success? That's a dream. For many, getting signed by a major record label is the be-all and end-all. What gradually sinks in – following some time being shafted by the varying machinations of the music industry – is the fact that out of thousands of bands knocking on the doors of record companies only a couple of dozen get signed in any given year. From this two dozen, about ten might make some money, and from this ten about half will have the semblance of a lengthy career. The wonderful/crazy thing here is that there seems to be an endless supply of hopefuls worryingly ready, willing and able to collectively prostrate themselves in front of the music industry so that they can be metaphorically whipped by cat-o'-nine-tails, humiliated and sneered at by smart-arsed music journalists, and shat upon by the very industry that a year previously had welcomed them with open arms. And still they arrive at the doors of record companies in their thousands. Sometimes, failure and ambition go hand in hand, and often the talent just isn't there to match aspiration. Sometimes, there truly are exceptionally talented people and bands that for whatever destiny-driven reasons don't make it. And sometimes, chancers get through the gates and forge a reasonably wealthy career out of dodgy dance moves, rigid smiles and cover versions. And so it goes.

❖

'The finest debut from an Irish band so far this year. The finest Irish pop album ever.'

*Excerpt of review of Blink's* A Map Of The Universe By Blink, *Olaf Tyaransen,* Hot Press *(10 August 1994)*

'Tuneless and hectoring and oh-so mannered. A few minutes of this is fairly interesting; 13 overlong, over-wrought songs is enough to make the sturdiest listener feel numb and queasy.'

*From review of Schtum's album,* Grow, Q *(May 1996)*

'Heavy-boned Paddies with forests of freckles have had a bad enough shake of it in London at the best of times, but this was a period when the sculpted cheekbones of Nick Rhodes [Duran Duran] and the sylph-like features of David Sylvian [Japan] were the modes du jour, not to mention the fact that style mags and club cliques had never exercised such a grip on the direction of pop before . . . Not to put too fine a point on it, Tokyo Olympics hadn't a fucking prayer once they moved [from Dublin to London]. When they put on slap and "trendy" gear . . . they looked like transvestite roadies, and there was still the problem of the bass player's moustache to contend with. Humiliating attendances on drizzly Tuesday nights in London's Rock Garden and other such insalubrious dens sapped the Olympics' spirit and such was the petering-out nature of their passing that they never even bothered to come back and say goodbye to us.'

*As part of the 'Worst Dublin Bands In The World . . . Ever' series, by George Byrne,* In Dublin *(19 December 1996)*

'I am after Chris de Burgh's ass.'

*Jody McStravick, former entrant in the 1982 Irish National Song Contest,* Hot Press *(24 December 1983)*

'I'm glad we got as far as we did and that we made at least one album that meant a lot to the people from the same background as us. But I wished I'd worked a lot harder. Looking back, compared to the way I'm living now, it seems there was an awful lot of time spent messing about; not confronting what had to be done and being too much a prisoner of the environment, especially in London, where there was that complete insistence of the album/tour/album nonsense. In hindsight, nothing ever really gelled sufficiently to make it seem as if it was worth our while being governed by that work ethic. It was not as productive as it could have been by a long, long way.'

*Cathal Coughlan on Microdisney,* The Irish Times *(July 2002)*

'Chicks Dig Scars welcomes you to Wormhole's cluttered bedsit. Showing off their four-chord capabilities, they inevitably turn up the lights, tread on a stale pizza and blow it.'

Q *(October 1995)*

'The notorious Puppy Love Bomb t-shirt? Christ, what was it – "Dublin Is Dead" or something like that. Yeah, the t-shirt was more popular than the band!'

*Marc Carroll, of The Hormones and formerly Puppy Love Bomb,* In Dublin *(12 September 1996)*

'It's almost a contradiction in terms that someone like me, who just wants to make music, has to deal with people whose only motivation is money. But we'll struggle on because we believe in what we're doing. I grew up in a time when traditional music and rock were both blossoming, but in different directions, and in my lifetime I've seen them crossover successfully, and I believe that Scullion have played a part in that. We're proud of what we've done and stand over it one hundred per cent. If

Carol is a hit, it'll be just one more chapter in a career that heretofore has been a catalogue of stops and starts.'
*Philip King,* Hot Press *(20 October 1988)*

'Ferghal McKee's sneers would be arrogance or misogyny if they weren't aimed as much at his own folly as the world's. The band have the power and dynamics to drive McKee's explorations to frightening heights of romantic intensity . . . This kind of intensity is a rarity these days, which is why Whipping Boy could and should be huge.'
Q *(December 1995)*

'Great things were expected of Bagatelle . . . and when they were taken on board by Polydor UK, sent in with Elton John's producer Gus Dudgeon and appeared on [BBC's] *Wogan*, they seemed about to crack it. Except, of course, that the middle-aged [BBC] Radio 2 audience across the water weren't completely brain dead and could see through a thinly disguised surrogate Elton John scam, minus the melodic invention, decent lyrics, visual flamboyance and sexual deviance. Having blown their big break, Bagatelle returned to playing ballrooms, and [lead singer] Liam Reilly developed a sulk which made Paul Brady look like Anthea Turner.'
*As part of the 'Worst Dublin Bands In The World . . . Ever'*
*series, by George Byrne,* In Dublin *(2 January 1997)*

'The [Bankrobbers] had been unhappy with their treatment by the EMI label, and felt they weren't offered the assistance they needed. Seamus O'Neill [drummer] explains, "EMI didn't want to know us, there was no support. They wouldn't even buy us a guitar, they just wouldn't back us at all." This lack of support was instrumental in Seamus leaving the band in 1983. He adds, "We signed a crap deal, we were given this dump of a house in Kensal Green where even the mice had rent books. I just thought, the label is either behind us or they're not. So I left." The band dissolved in 1984 when their contract with EMI expired. After the band split, Joby [Fox, bassist] formed Energy Orchard with ex-members of another Good Vibrations band, 10 Past 7, who had among their ranks a young Brian Kennedy. Seamus stayed in London and started touring production with Level 42 . . . On 28 November 2002, The Bankrobbers reformed for a one-off charity gig at the Empire in Belfast . . . They played four numbers that included "Jenny" and "All Night Long", and got an incredible reception. On the back of that appearance they have been offered numerous festival spots but all have declined.'

It Makes You Want To Spit *(Reekus Music 2003)*

'As part of their Band of '89 winnings, Just A Philistine will be cominatcha soon with a waxing to be distributed by Record Services, U2's distribution company. As yet it hasn't been decided what format the disc will take or what songs it will feature. What it definitely won't be, JAP assure me, is "a nice, radio-friendly single."'

*Damian Corless reports on the winners of the Carling/Hot Press Band of '89,* Hot Press *(21 September 1989)*

'Looking back I'm very proud of how idealistic we managed to stay. I love what we did; we didn't imitate what was fashionable at the time, which was probably some bad sub-U2 band getting money thrown at them. We sent the first tape, *Songs for Swinging Celibates,* to [one- time U2-owned] Mother Records, with a letter asking for £500 so that we could bring the album out on vinyl. We told them we didn't want a record deal, just a helping hand – I mean, U2 set the label up to help Irish bands, didn't they? We received a letter back saying that we were too original and that they didn't know what to do with us. We put "too original" on posters after that.'

*Toasted Heretics' lead singer and novelist Julian Gough,* The Irish Times *(November 2005)*

'It's more than ironic that [Skid Row] a band named after the areas of American cities frequented by alcoholics and drug addicts should be fronted by a man who'd never let any substance stronger than tea infiltrate his system, but over the years Brendan "Brush" Shiels emerged as a man with more contradictions than a Fine Gael seminar on "openness and clarity".

*As part of the 'Worst Dublin Bands In The World . . . Ever' series, by George Byrne,* In Dublin *(3 February 1997)*

'Their one and only single, "I Can Make The Future", was released in 1980, with the B-side, "Australia", actually showing more promise and being more immediate. Katmandu then did the TV shows and all the

# Rockaganda

Dublin venues – The Sportsman's Inn, Sallynoggin Inn, McGonagles and, of course, their residency in The Baggot. The pressure of paying the rent by continuous gigging, not having a record contract and having precious little time to write, led to a growing frustration amongst members, and by late '81 the band decided to call it a day. Their last gig was immortalized by [lead singer, Marty] Lundy's reluctance to leave the gents toilet, singing the whole gig there via radio mike.'

It Makes You Want To Spit *(Reekus Music 2003)*

'An outfit with a shaky deal, a frontman with delusions of artistry but no singing voice, a guitarist more suited to contributing sound effects to sci-fi movies than playing songs . . . And an all-pervading atmosphere of of misplaced star status and stupidity. On the latter front, the band secured themselves an unimpeachable place in the annals of Rock Idiocy when the normally stable (drummer) Wayne Sheehy decided that his percussive arsenal wasn't complete enough for the sonic complexities of Cactus World News compositions so he added . . . A Kosangas bottle. Yep, there it was, a fucking Kosangas bottle sprayed black to match the rest of the kit and suspended by chains in what looked like a tubular steel door-frame. The end could not be far away.'

*As part of the 'Worst Dublin Bands In The World . . . Ever'*
*series, by George Byrne,* In Dublin *(24 October 1996)*

'It's because rock 'n' roll stops that it exists. Don't grasp it, let it clasp you to its huge heart and when it does make love to you, fuck it and smile and kiss it goodbye because, baby, you'll feel it again in heaven. With the (Golden) Horde, if it wasn't there, then it wasn't worth it for us. We worked to get it all high, to feel the life in a room and all around us. A circus, a party, a flight, a fight, I loved a crowd as much as I loved anyone. And the beat that was in our hearts was the beat that was in the air. Whatever you felt was real, believe me. Empathy may be the highest part of what it is to be human, leading us all to our aim – joy, communion, truth, noise, youth. A real party has to end, only the fake ones go on forever. By playing our life away, we got it on, no fear, no favours. Baby, you wanted it and so did we. We drank a lot of wine and we kissed a lot of girls and made a lot of noise and we did baby. Hail Hail Rock 'n' Roll!'

*Press release from Simon Carmody, lead singer of The Golden Horde, on their decision to split up, (20 April 1994)*

# BLESS ME, FATHER – THE ROCK STAR'S CONFESSIONAL

If you're looking for light relief, move on. Of all the sections in this handy, pocket-sized, remarkably affordable, extremely insightful book, this is the most serious. All manner of Irish rock stars speak coherently and intelligently on the true nature of their characters. From Sinéad O'Connor's excoriating exposé of family and love to Bob Geldof's ever-honest accounts of life, the universe and everything; from Damien Rice's relationship with his mistakes to Aslan's Christy Dignam's relationship with hard drugs; from Snow Patrol's Gary Lightbody's self-loathing to Róisín Murphy's desire to be a bit more of a – well, when you read it you'll understand.

'I did it out of desperation. Peter [Gabriel] was the person I was closest to and I was trying to convince him to go out with me when he didn't really want to. I needed him as a father, not as a lover. He didn't want to have anything to do with me because I was such an emotional roller-coaster and this hurt me so much, because I was in a bad way. It was all awful. We went to the MTV Awards and he went off with all these glamorous women because all these glamorous women are always queuing up to shag him, and then there was going to be a three-day period when I was going to be by myself because there was no gig and I couldn't face it so I wanted to go to sleep, but I said to God in my mind, whatever God is, I said, I don't care if I die. I took a load of sleeping tablets and bottle of vodka and I passed out. Then Peter and a hotel security man came in and all I could hear suddenly was, Is there a pulse? And I'm inside myself saying, Fucking hell, there is! I'm here!'

*Sinéad O'Connor,* Q *(September 1994)*


'The hardest thing before was I was afraid to come home, because there was nothing to come home to. All the money in the world isn't going to get you love. You get to a point where you need real love. And real people.'

*Dolores O'Riordan,* Cara Magazine *(March 2002)*


'How I've seen myself over the past thirty years has been as a ruthless individualist, an experimenter. I'm one of these people who has been given a very broad palette of stylistic capabilities, and as often as not that has been a problem for me, a liability. Other artists are very one dimensional, so they have little choice and are accordingly more focussed than I am. I would see myself as someone who always felt there was something else I had to learn and to discover. I've always liked trying different things, and been more interested in having glorious failures than being really predictable.'

*Paul Brady,* Cara Magazine *(November 1999)*

'You don't have to do anything you don't want to. That's what I'm learning. It's like photo shoots . . . I mean, I just feel like a knob. It's like, I don't feel that special. I don't feel that talented. I know singers and guitar players who are much better than me. I like the songs that I write . . . But I only write them and do what I do out of being a complete dick in life, in a way. I love being left alone to make all the mistakes I make without anyone watching me or judging it. That's what I love about being a musician . . . You can fuck up, then when you're down you can heal yourself with a song, or heal a situation or a person, and then people take it into their lives.'

*Damien Rice,* Hot Press *(24 September 2003)*

'I had plans for my life and they certainly did not involve fame. I wanted to go to university and study theology. Then "Nothing Compares 2 U" took off and I was suddenly very famous. I'd grown up in an extremely violent, abusive atmosphere and I was utterly susceptible to outside influences. The way I think about it is that I stepped out of one version of hell and into the music business – which is just a glitzier version of hell. I felt utterly alone.'

*Sinéad O'Connor,* Uncut *(July 2007)*

'1985 [and Live Aid] was a massive dash to set up an organisation that would handle that influx of money and distribute it on a national basis. That was frightening: if we'd fucked it up it would have been completely catastrophic, in damaging the people we were meant to help and betraying those who helped. So there was a terrible sense of terror, before the concert, of it going hideously wrong. I'd never believed in the idea of a "cold sweat" before, but waking up I'd be really freezing . . . There was a terror of failure. Let's imagine the simple fact of no one turning up: 15 hours of The Boomtown Rats would have been a little hard to take . . . And what if there wasn't any money? I'd look a complete fucking idiot.'

*Bob Geldof, Q (January 1990)*

'When I was a child I was abused on two different occasions by people. I was raped when I was six and it happened again when I was ten. I thought I had something to do with that and I blocked it out. And what it did was that it threw my sexuality into question. In myself. It happened with two men so my whole idea of male acceptance was totally fucked around . . . so I took drugs to block out the emotional turmoil.'

*Aslan's Christy Dignam, Hot Press (20 April 1989)*

'The denim jacket and check shirt have become like a stigmata to me . . . I've toured too much for my own good. It hasn't left time for very much else, unfortunately. You don't develop any family life and it makes relationships very difficult. There's always a certain percentage missing from your life. As a human being you only have so much to give, not just in terms of your physical body but in how you deal with people.'

*Rory Gallagher, as quoted in* Mojo *(October 1998)*

'Thin Lizzy were successful, the pressure was off and I was having fun, but after four or five months I was doing myself in, drinking and high on the whole thing. I was really committed to Thin Lizzy and spent half the time on stage on my knees or back, going crazy and playing as flash as I can, often unable to get back up again. I needed discipline and a direction that would get me out of the rut of the typical rock guitarist's self-destructive streak I had at the time.'

*Gary Moore, Q (April 1992)*

'I'm a manic depressive . . . I didn't get diagnosed until a couple of years ago, but I was running around trying to find out what was going on for years. I was kind of not quite depressed until I was about twenty-two, twenty-three, and then I was fucking suicidal until about two years ago . . . It's very hard to live with and can take a long time to get properly diagnosed. So I had gone for therapy when I was twenty-eight and [been] diagnosed with regular depression. But that actually wasn't the case and anti-depressants are

very bad for people with manic depression, so everything got a little . . . skewed. So thank God I finally got diagnosed properly and got proper treatment. But that's what I was doing in rehab. I've never had a drug or drink problem, other than I'm a fucking major chronic spliffhead.'
*Sinéad O'Connor,* Mojo *(October 2005)*

'[Depression] comes and goes. It's like the weather . . . There's sunny weather and there's calm weather. When you go into the storm you think you're never going to get out again. I hit rock-bottom about three years ago. I just felt completely lost. I didn't know where I was going or what I was doing. Then I came out of it and realised it was great to be alive no matter what.'
*Johnny Duhan,* Hot Press *(7 September 1984)*

'It seems to me that the purpose of life is life, and afterwards oblivion. I had this argument with the Dalai Lama. I said, why go through the purgatory of rebirth? He had to have purgatory translated and when it was translated he broke his hole laughing. I said, I don't want to come back as a parrot. If you give me billions, I wouldn't re-live one second of my life. I don't want to go through it again.'
*Bob Geldof,* Q *(November 1992)*

'I'm a moodswing woman: happy one minute, depressed the next. Ho ho.'
*Dolores O'Riordan,* Q *(May 1996)*

# Rockaganda

'I probably am one of the most vulnerable people you'll ever meet. I project tough as a defence mechanism. I always was too defensive, so I go on the offensive to guard myself. Mostly because I am totally lacking in self-confidence in most areas of my life. I know I can sing well, but even that I had to be convinced of. Yet it is my decision and my right to project an image that protects me. If people can't see beyond that that's their problem. But I will hide that side of my nature as much as I can because I really, really don't want to be hurt anymore.'

*Mary Coughlan,* Hot Press *(22 March 1990)*

'We go for walks, and I pick up the groceries from the local supermarket. I don't go down the road driving a Ferrari in my Gucci slippers. What you see is what you get – a fairly focused, solid, grounded person. That's me.'

*Ronan Keating,* Cara Magazine *(March 2001)*

'I find desperation an attractive quality in others but not in myself. I'm certainly compelled towards something and it's never satisfied.'

*Bob Geldof,* Q *(January 1995)*

'I come from a working class background, but I'm still the same as when I started. One of my big lessons in life is don't buy bullshit and don't pay lip-service to it. If you're like me, there's nothing to battle against, because you're already there, just be yourself. It's not going to change and you're not going to fit into it, you can't fit into it, stalemate, just relax and be yourself, that's all you can do, just be yourself. Get off the cross!'

*Van Morrison,* Q *(August 1993)*

'I want to thank everybody and to say sorry for breaking Thin Lizzy up. I wish we could have continued more than people realise – in a way I feel I've let everybody down, but remember I'm not as a hard as I'm made out to be.'

*Thin Lizzy's Phil Lynott, writing in the programme notes to the final band shows in Ireland, as quoted in* Mojo *(February 2006)*

'I just find it hard to be a so-called pop star. It conflicts with creativity. You're expected to be at certain places at certain times and do certain things. Which is contrary to the muse. I mean, you just get it when you get it.'

*Van Morrison, as quoted in* Can You Feel The Silence? A New Biography of Van Morrison *by Clinton Heylin (Viking Books 2002)*

'I simply do not have the ability to be dishonest. I just wish I had been a happier person back then . . . I regret having been so unhappy, for failing to fill that gaping hole in myself.'

*Sinéad O'Connor,* Uncut *(July 2007)*

'I've had a lot of opportunities to make money out of the music industry. There was the vacancy with Marillion – I turned that down. Trevor Horn [record producer] wanted to do a Paul Young vibe with me, where he'd pick out classic songs, write a couple of songs together and do the typical Trevor Horn production job. That would have made me a fuckin' fortune. But it was never about that with me. At the back of my mind I always know I'd have to go up to me Ma's house where I'm going to see guys I grew up with, people who will definitely see through any bullshit. And I swear to God, it bothers me that people would think that I'd sell myself like that. I just want people to think that whatever I did – good, bad or indifferent – I'd mean it.'

*Aslan's Christy Dignam, D'Side (August/September 1994)*

'I wish I could relax and go, whatever, with life. I'll get the hang of it. I have to be a bit more of a cunt to be a really good pop star.'

*Róisín Murphy, Q (September, 2000)*

'There's the desire not to be this huge star, and on the other hand I enjoy the trappings, getting into discos free, because I'm not so removed from the normal that I don't get a buzz out of that. I'm not so cool yet that I haven't lost that. I wish sometimes that I had.'

*Bob Geldof, NME (20 October 1979)*

'When you live with the Devil you learn there's a God very quickly. I say it with love and it's all over and my mother's dead and all that, but she was a fucking monster. I found music in me quite young and I was a religious little person and that's what saved my ass. I was crap at everything else. I never did anything at school, never wrote in a book . . . So thank God I found music. In those days in Ireland, too, there was no such thing as therapy. You didn't tell anyone that you were fucked up in the head or you were depressed.'

*Sinéad O'Connor,* Mojo *(October 2005)*


'The first eight years were dark and peppered with horrible incidents. People see this happy-go-lucky guy, and I am. But it's fair to say I've been a fucking arsehole at times, too. We made two albums and then we were dropped. At that point I went off the rails. I was in a mess and I was ruining the band. I went to pieces. I thought world domination wasn't far away and it would happen like that (snaps fingers) Little did I know you have to have good songs and be good live. I didn't really realise that we didn't have the songs . . . I started drinking. I was being an arsehole. I was swearing at people, smashing equipment and acting like a dickhead. I loathed myself. I thought the band was over and the life I wanted had passed me by. You wouldn't have wanted to have met the 25-year-old me.'

*Gary Lightbody (Snow Patrol),* Q *(April 2007)*


'[The glass] is always half-full now, not half-empty any more. I had some difficulties with fame and my life as a young woman, but now I just feel very blessed to be here and to have my family and be sane.'

*Dolores O'Riordan,* Mojo *(June 2007)*

## Rockaganda

'Being in London did have its compensations. Jesus loves a sinner and there's no point in having a confessional if you're not going to do something you have to confess. So London offered a beautiful opportunity for me to become a disgrace.'

*Shane MacGowan,* Mojo *(September 2004)*